LOVE IT OR OR LEAVE IT?

A DIALOG ON LOYALTY

by ERLING JORSTAD

AUGSBURG PUBLISHING HOUSE
Minneapolis, Minnesota

LOVE IT OR LEAVE IT?

To E. Clifford Nelson
teacher, critic, friend

CONTENTS

PREFACE

In a few hundred years cultural anthropologists will ponder over a unique American tribal rite of the late 20th century — the bumper sticker. The terse, blunt wording of the slogans may suggest how bitterly the inhabitants of this once promised land regarded their enemies.

AMERICA, LOVE IT OR LEAVE IT! *and*
AMERICA, LOVE IT AND LIVE IT!

VICTORY NOW OVER COMMUNISM! *and*
HOW MANY SHOPPING DAYS LEFT UNTIL PEACE?

GO TO COLLEGE, LEARN TO RIOT! *and*
LIBERATE THE SCHOOLS!

LAW AND ORDER, THE AMERICAN WAY! *and*
POWER TO THE PEOPLE!

NO NORTH VIETNAMESE EVER CALLED ME NIGGER!
and
SAVE THE NEIGHBORHOOD SCHOOLS!

SAVE THE SEVEN! *and*
SUPPORT YOUR LOCAL POLICE!

HELL, NO! WE WON'T GO! *and*
HONOR THE FLAG!

Our anthropologists may not be able to understand any better than we do what all this means. They probably will conclude, as we do, that "something went wrong with America." The researchers will have, however, the benefit of knowing how it ended.

This book may not be of any help to those in future millennia, but it does attempt to speak to those facing the complex issues of faith and loyalty in today's America. It centers on the question: why, after nearly two centuries of experience in self-government, including civil war, world wars, and depressions, are Americans still so bitterly divided over what constitutes "liberty and justice for all"? Carrying this a step farther, we must ask: can America maintain her cherished dedication to liberty and justice while its people keep dividing into increasingly hostile camps? And finally, we should consider: what resources are available for us to reestablish some minimum consensus as to what constitutes loyalty and patriotism? Does the Christian faith suggest some direction this nation may follow to prevent the escalating dissension of our times from erupting into perpetual violence?

This question is no longer an "interesting problem" for ivory tower coffee hours. Nor is the potential for violence simply the work of a minority of disgruntled misfits. Hard hats, clergymen, flower children, blacks, chicanos, pacifists, the young and old, housewives, Nobel prize winners, and millionaires all have risked physical violence in recent times to express their bitterness with the injustices of our world and nation.

One has only to look at Northern Ireland or Pakistan

or Nigeria, or recall Indonesia a few years ago, where a civil war led to more than 150,000 deaths, to understand what can happen when the populace cannot or will not find any workable consensus of ideals and norms under which they can live in peace. These events are happening, not in the benighted dark ages or medieval times or even a hundred years ago. They are a part of our immediate world. History may not "prove" anything except that no society can long exist unless its people share at least a minimum standard of liberty and justice for all.

Although the present hullabaloo over patriotism and loyalty may evaporate overnight, we have adequate reason to face this question as honestly as possible. The extent of physical violence, as an expression of moral outrage and political dissent, has soared rapidly in the 1960s. As Richard Hofstadter demonstrates, this is a sharp break with every other era of our past, except for the Civil War.[1] Those institutions which traditionally have represented order and stability in our nation, such as the police and parents, have been bitterly critcized. New ideas leading for reform advanced especially by colleges and universities have been ignored or discarded as irrelevant. Finally, the churches in their traditional role of mediator, or conciliator among varying groups in society, have undergone drastic internal upheavals in the past ten years, so that there is no common understanding of the mission of the church in today's world.

Beyond this, the polls show that about three-fourths of the Americans now believe that religion is losing its influence in this nation's public life. Add to that the decline in church membership and in church financial resources, plus growing clerical dropout, and it becomes clear that the winds of drastic change are indeed blowing across the land. Schools, churches, the family, and elected officials no longer command the respect and influence they once had in American life.

But nothing positive has yet filled this vacuum. Out of fear, outrage, and, at times boredom, those in all walks of life are making their demand on the "American

11

dream," demanding that it come true for them, and right now! If that means breaking the law, then that is what will have to be done!

Obviously no sane American *wants* the kind of violence that has gripped Northern Ireland or Pakistan. Yet an increasing number of citizens are willing to make their opinions known, even by direct force. And to compound the difficulties, each group seems content to stand in its own corner, shouting denunciations of the opposition, but not willing to call a truce for exploratory negotiations. Rarely if ever in American history has each faction been so totally and uncritically convinced of the absolute rightness of its particular cause. Each has its own special revelation, as expressed in the lapel button: "Love Me or I'll Clobber You."

Now is the time to take stock of the crises we seem so skilled at creating, and in turn to see why older traditions that held this nation together now seem so shaky. The first half of this book attempts to redefine the resources of the Judeo-Christian tradition and the resources from the American past which have shaped our understanding of loyalty and patriotism. The historical perspective serves as the springboard into a more detailed examination of the manner in which Americans have expressed loyalty to their nation in religious terms by creating something very close to a "civil religion" out of democracy. This shared consensus of nationalist-religious convictions served the great majority of Americans well until about the mid 1960s when dissent, then protest, and then violence erupted into view.

Chapter 4 attempts to outline the specific areas of conflict as these emerged out of the polarization of public opinion about the understanding of liberty and justice. The specific issues included here are welfare, minority rights, student dissent, the draft, activist clergy, the flag, and the Pentagon Papers. These are not the only major issues in dispute but they constitute perhaps the most immediate and visible areas of our bitter divisions. I will not pretend to offer the one and only Christian solution to any of these disputes. What I intend in the historical and theological sections, Chapters 1-4, is to help identify disputes and explain *why* the disputes defined in Chapter 5 are so serious today. Hopefully this study will encourage readers to participate in further discussions. Workable solutions may not always emerge out of the open exchange of viewpoints, but in the United States of America no one would settle for any other method.

RESOURCES: BIBLICAL AND THEOLOGICAL

1

Not every American today who demonstrates, waves the flag, or speaks his mind finds his guidance in the Bible. Furthermore, in nations such as Northern Ireland those in direct conflict with one another claim the sanction of Scripture for their side alone. All of which is to say that the Bible cannot be used as an infallible solution to every man-made problem, such as conflicting loyalties. Nor was it intended to be such a guide.

Yet the two testaments offer resources for the perspective of transcendence, the starting point for any discussion of divided loyalty. God stands as judge over all nations, over all history, and over all competing rivalries of man. No nation or economic system can be raised to the position of being beyond criticism or beyond the need for reform. To deify any system would be to fall

15

into the snare of idolatry, and to ignore the ultimate source of authority, God's sovereignty over his creation.

The expression of God's transcendence is the Incarnation, God revealing himself in Jesus. His life and ministry make concrete the will of God concerning loyalty and the power of the state. Keep in mind the fact that the Jewish people, chosen to bring forth the Messiah, were living under the occupational army of Rome, which had its own state religion. Jesus laid down two principles: "You shall love the Lord your God with all your heart, and with all your soul, and with all your mind," and the second, "You shall love your neighbor as yourself." He used the parable of the Good Samaritan as his illustration of who is the neighbor.

This means that ultimate loyalty is due only to the one God, not to tribal or national deities, or to anything less than the transcendent God of creation. God is the judge of all man-made governments and societies. This also means that God rules over the one eternal kingdom, which though transcendent is yet a part of the believer's everyday life: "thy kingdom come on earth as it is in heaven." That petition accepts the presence of governments here on earth and at the same time points the believer to the final kingdom. In other words, Jesus is not denying the presence and the power of the earthly kingdoms; he makes no attempt in these teachings to overthrow all forms of civil government.

But Rome, of course, wanted no divided loyalty from her citizens or from the Jewish people; allegiance was due only to the state and to no other institution. As a result, many scholars believe, Rome had to execute Jesus when its leaders feared, not his ethical teachings, but the possibility that he might create subversive activity among the Jews in winning their loyalty to the kingdom he was preaching.

One final teaching of Jesus remains to be incorporated here, one which has been misinterpreted and misapplied over the centuries, that quotation from Jesus in Matthew 22:17-21, "Then pay Caesar what is due to Caesar and pay God what is due to God" (NEB). This does *not* mean the realm of government is totally distinct from that of ecclesiastical concern. It does mean Jesus recognized the need for temporal government and the legitimacy of certain of its demands on the citizens. These demands in no manner force a believer to compromise his ultimate loyalty to the kingdom of God.

This means that no form of government is illegitimate unless it forbids its citizens to pay to God what is his: the guarantee of protection under law that each citizen has the full and free expression of his religion as his right. When a government forbids that, the believer's ultimate loyalty leads him to resist.

The next resource in the New Testament for understanding divided loyalty is found in the writings of the apostles and St. Paul. After Pentecost, the disciples in Jerusalem soon found the Roman officials wanted no part of their preaching of the Christian faith. They were ordered into court, where they stated, "We must obey God rather than man (Acts 5:29). Like the "pay to Caesar" text, this passage has been used to justify a multitude of both noble and sinful deeds. As Peter and John intended this statement, however, it was limited to their belief that they must be given the opportunity to preach, and that the political order had no authority to stop them. Any other reading of this passage is the product of the reader's imagination.

It was St. Paul who defined the Christian dimensions of the problems facing Christian converts living under Roman law. For one thing, Paul was the first leader to open the gates of membership to Gentiles. In Galatians 3:28 ("There is neither Jew nor Greek. . . .") he lays down the principle that the Christian church is to be free of distinctions based on race or nationality. It is open to all who believe. Paul realized that the new life in Christ raised crucial questions for believers. For example: should they practice slavery? was a Roman marriage valid? He chose to work out a solution from a conservative stance: "there is no authority except from God, and those that exist have been instituted by God" (Romans 13:1). This does not sanction divine right of kings, contrary to what

James I of England believed. It does show Paul did not want to anger the Roman army, which could have wiped out his tiny band of believers at its whim. In similar fashion, Paul told slaves to obey their masters and wives to obey their husbands (1 Cor. 11:2 ff). For our understanding of loyalty, Paul established here the principle of the believers' duty to cooperate with established political authorities when such association did not compromise their faith.

In Romans 13:1-7 "the most extended and most positive discussion anywhere in the New Testament of Christian duty to civil government" is presented, according to Daniel Stevick.[1] The crucial verse reads, "Let every person be subjected to the governing authorities. For there is no authority except from God, and those that exist have been instituted by God." Again, Paul states that God is the source of all authority, and thus the Christian is to obey those authorities who rule according to the order God has established. But, Stevick suggests, this was not a "universal law" Paul was establishing for all times under all conditions. For instance, he knew nothing of the Nazis when he wrote that passage. What seems to be the best interpretation here is that so long as the rulers establish and enforce laws which follow the moral order of God, having been established through conscience and the commands of Scripture, the citizens are obeying God by obeying these laws. The decisive point is that civil government as such is not necessarily evil nor necessarily the perfect instrument for God's will on earth.

Elsewhere, for example, Paul cautions Christians to be alert to possible usurpations of this moral order by earthly rulers for evil purposes. In 1 Corinthians 6 he counsels the Christians not to bring their own disputes into Roman courts of law. He obviously is stating the courts are devoid of authority in matters relating directly to Christians. In this sense, he expresses the teaching of Jesus regarding the distinctive jurisdictions of the heavenly and earthly kingdoms.

In summary, loyalty to civil rulers is required on those

matters which pertain to the issues of daily life and make orderly society possible. But disobedience to unjust or immoral laws is also a part of the Christian's loyalty. By making resistance *against* evil civil authority, the Christian is expressing his love *for* God. That is what Paul and the early Christians did in their resistance to Roman authority.

LUTHER AND CALVIN

Skipping over the teachings of the early church fathers, we need to consider what Luther and Calvin taught concerning the relationship of the Christian to the state. Far more than Calvin, Luther would leave the civil realm to stand under the judgment of God, freed from direct political controls by the church leaders. Luther asked that the churches be given complete freedom to pursue their work, and in turn the Lutheran leaders would not insist on telling the princes of Germany how to govern their states.

Obviously, Luther taught that the church did offer spiritual and moral guidance to civil authorities. Contrary to some critics, he did not teach that any and all laws must be obeyed. He did insist, however, that the primary concern of the believer was justification by grace through faith. Such grace was sacramental in nature and thus beyond the authority or scope of civil authority. Putting it another way, Luther rejected the idea that an explicitly Christian political order could ever be created by man. That is the essence of his outlook and cannot be emphasized too strongly. No political party, no political "ism," no economic structure could ever explicitly reflect God's authority. Man was too sinful, too subject to his pride and selfish impulses ever to overcome self interest in any of his relationships with others. Hence the churches must act as the guardians of Christian standards of conduct, and must constantly preach the Word as found in the Bible. When the believer followed that standard of loyalty, the temporal demands on him by civil government would fall into proper perspective.[2]

However, America was not founded by Lutherans. It

was founded by Calvinists of several persuasions, and that fact has been monumentally decisive in shaping the relationships between Christianity and Americanism down to our day.

Sharing in Luther's belief in original sin, Calvin chose to emphasize the absolutely sovereign will of God. This he defined as unlimited power and total control over every phase of human activity from the beginning of time until its consummation. Every institution, including civil government, was a part of this preordained order of God. Since man's sole purpose in life was the preparation of his soul for the hereafter, every institution including civil government must help prepare him for that supreme life in eternity. Government existed not only for the obvious tasks of maintaining civil order, but to help make men morally good. Alone man was so corrupt as to be unable to establish any right Christian conduct. But with explicit Christian authority defining and governing his social life he was able to discipline his energies as he prepared for his eternal destiny.

Putting it another way, Calvin put into practice in Geneva his conviction that every institution in society must reflect and enforce the will of God against the innately sinful will of man. This required strong leadership. Instead of leaving this to the princes as did Luther, Calvin established a government by the "elect," the visible saints, who by education, piety, and leadership demonstrated their ability to rule in harmony with God's will. They so directed every phase of society as to coerce the citizens, even the non-believers, into obeying their commands. To them this was not persecution but simply a recognition that God's standards for human conduct were extremely high and could be met, even partially, only by the most dedicated and disciplined efforts of the populace.

Calvin took this one step further. Conceding that sin would continue to influence man's judgment and behavior until death, he emphasized that the indwelling power of God among Christians could create something very close to an authentic Christian commonwealth.

This was demonstrated by his work in Geneva. Contrary to Luther, then, the Calvinist tradition argued that explicitly Christian forms of government and of economic and social institutions could be created, enforced, and extended to other communities. It was that conviction that influenced the English Puritans to believe they could create a Bible Commonwealth, or a Puritan Zion in the New World, in which the will of God would reign in all its majesty and truth.

THE PURITANS

At this point, the issue of divided loyalty for Christians becomes more clear. The Puritans who came to New England insisted that everyone who chose to reside within their political jurisdiction was welcome so long as he obeyed all the laws of the government. Since the Puritans believed their doctrines and ethical practices were as harmonious with the will of God as was humanly possible, they found no reason to practice religious freedom in their community. To do so would be to admit they were not concerned with maintaining the purity and justice of God's ordinances. In other words, loyalty to the civil government was equivalent to loyalty to God; the Puritans made no distinctions between the two. One need not fear having to disobey unjust laws, as counselled by Paul for instance, because the Puritans had only just laws. Thus, obedience to the laws that existed was one form of expressing love of God and of preparing the soul for the life to come.

The key to our understanding comes from this perspective: the original interpretation among Americans concerning loyalty to God and to the state was Calvinistic rather than Lutheran. A believer could speak with confidence about the Christian position on charging interest, divorce, inheritance laws, regulation of gambling and alcohol, the education of youth, and a host of related issues. The civil government, according to its original form in New England, exists not only to protect property and prevent crime, but it exists to help make men morally good. The citizenry knows what this standard of good is because God has revealed it to them. To live up to these standards of righteousness, the citizen in obeying the civil authorities is obeying God. He does not have a divided loyalty. These regulations are subject to change and improvement, but so long as they harmonize with the revealed will of God, they constitute the authority the government needs to govern the populace.

Putting it another way, the Puritans believed that their society must not only stand *against* specific evils, but also that it must stand *for* specific codes of behavior and specific ideals. The achievement of the goals is what government is all about. Thus it is justified in using coercion, and punishment if necessary, to carry out this mandate. This conviction that explicit Christian norms and beliefs, not corrupted by man's sinful judgment, are the proper business of the American people furnishes us the continuity we need to move from the New Testament up through Luther, Calvin, and the Puritans.

Richard Hofstadter wrote that of all the nations in the world, "the United States began with perfection and aspired to progress." The major themes of that vision are the topics for our next chapter.

THE AMERICAN CREED

2

From the beginning of its history, the United States has been regarded as a unique nation. Foreign travellers and residents alike have attempted to understand what it is that constitutes this distinctive dimension of the national character. Gunnar Myrdal, the Swedish sociologist, well defined this as the "American Creed," a "basic homogeneity and stability" of ideals which Americans of all national origins, classes, regions, creeds, and colors have in common, and which most have accepted as valid.[1] What we survey in this chapter are the major ingredients of this creed, those landmark expressions of shared values and ideals which have constituted the essence of "Americanism."

This list does not pretend to be exhaustive, and exceptions can be made to every generalization. But we need to define that *useable past* which Americans today are claiming as their own and the rationale for the demands they are making. All groups — hawks and doves, segregationists and integrationists, social gospelers and fundamentalists — all are appealing to the American Creed. Therefore we need to understand it with some precision.

THE CITY ON A HILL

As early as 1630 American colonists were talking about the unique character of their new land. This was not to be one more trading post to enhance the wealth of the mother country. The New World was to be the new Eden for true believers, that unsullied land where God had led the Puritans to start afresh in building the kingdom on earth. God had withheld this land from the Christians until this moment in history, the Puritans believed, because he was now telling mankind what he expected of them in this new act of redemption.

Two distinct themes emerge from this concept. First, the Puritans believed God was fully directing all of their activities. He was in complete control of the entire enterprise. Thus they dare not shirk or give less than their supreme effort lest they be judged unwilling to live up to the high standards God had established for his elect. Second, Massachusetts was to "be as a Citty Upon a Hill, the eies of all people are uppon us." This new society was unlike anything before in God's providence. By succeeding in the New World the Puritans would show everyone that their society was in fact based on the eternal truth of God's Word.

Note the Calvinist underpinnings here. The United States was founded by those who believed they were creating a totally Christian society, one freed from the corruptions of the Old World and dedicated to preserving those truths which God had revealed to them. This sense of being a chosen people, of travelling through extreme hardships as did the Israelites in the desert, inspired the Puritans to regard themselves as starting a new chapter in history. Since every energy was directed towards enhancing the success of the colony, every responsible citizen was demonstrating his loyalty to God by being loyal to the community. This was simply the will of God.

"WORK FOR THE NIGHT IS COMING"

Although the tightly controlled Puritan Zion around Boston gradually mellowed into peaceful coexistence with non-church members, American colonists persisted in their conviction that God indeed had some special destiny for them. The very fact that they had overcome severe economic and personal hardship and had turned the 13 colonies into prospering societies was the proof they needed to convince themselves of God's special concern for them.

As the population increased and the economy became more stable, the colonists found themselves faced with the age-old question of the relationship between godliness and the acquisition of wealth. Jesus had said some strong things to the rich young ruler who asked about that problem and went away "sorrowfully sad." There was also that verse about rich men, needle's eyes, and camels.

A second basic ingredient in the American Creed emerged out of the colonial resolution of this question, a solution generally referred to as the "Puritan" or "Protestant Ethic." We need not here take up the question raised by Max Weber of which came first, Protestantism or capitalism. But we do want to define this doctrine in the American Creed. The Puritans concluded God had placed them on earth and had given them the resources and talents for physical survival. But he had not made the earning of one's livelihood very easy. Rather, he challenged men to develop their talents, turn two into four, and thus gain dominion over the earth. By responding constructively to God's command, the Christian who worked hard, invested or saved his surplus, showed initiative and ingenuity in opening new fields of endeav-

or, was in fact worshipping God just as much as when he was in Sunday services.

Conversely, and this is decisive for today's issue on public welfare, God not only demanded hard work, he punished those who were the drones in the beehive. Those who followed his commands *could not help but succeed* since they were following God's orders. But those who ignored these commands would remain poor and dependent. Thus was developed the classic American idea that to be poor was a sin because one was not utilizing his God-given talents.

To the Puritan, America had become a prosperous land because of the hard work, ingenuity, and self-discipline of those willing to pay the price in surrendering creature comforts and fleshly gratification. Beyond that, they knew they must "work for the night is coming." They had this one opportunity to prove to God they were worthy of his election to eternal bliss. They dare not let him down by accomplishing anything less in life than the highest degree of economic success.

This can be stated another way. Because of the challenge of developing the vast resources of the frontier, and from the sanction bestowed by Calvinist ethics to capitalist enterprise, Americans became achievement minded. They measured their own worth in terms of their material accomplishments. This they believed was a fair means for evaluation. Everyone had an equal opportunity to succeed in this country; there was no landed aristocracy or professional military or clerical class to uphold the old, unjust system of rank and privilege. Thus those who did succeed here were those who had done it on their own initiative.

Out of this came a unique American concept. There is always room here for someone willing to work, and so long as he follows the basic rules of honesty and respect for others, he cannot help but succeed. By the opposite token, those who are poor have deliberately chosen that level of life for themselves, and should be allowed to live that way since that is the decision they made for themselves. They could improve their situation if they wanted. But since they are lazy, they should be allowed to enjoy their indolence.

"ENDOWED BY THEIR CREATOR WITH CERTAIN INALIENABLE RIGHTS"

The third major theme in the American Creed was nobly summarized by Thomas Jefferson in the Declaration of Independence. Americans were claiming the right of independence from Britain not only because of unjust taxes and unrepresentative political bodies, but because it was the will of God. This concept was a predictable conclusion from the Puritan sense of divine destiny and the success Americans had known in developing their own institutions before 1776. They concurred with the statement that the right to life, liberty, and the pursuit of happiness was not only self-evident to intelligent men. This right was the work of God who had established this form of civil order for mankind. The Declaration explicitly recognized the transcendent origins of human liberty. This conviction gave the rebellious colonists the absolute authority they needed to claim the right and *duty* of revolution to protect themselves against tyrannical government.

Political liberty was not merely something "nice" for mankind. It was God's will and was "inalienable"; it could not be taken away by any human authority whatever. That statement summarized the whole thrust of the American Creed as being the expression of God's will. By being loyal to their natural rights, the colonists were being loyal to God.

In his famous pamphlet, *Common Sense,* Tom Paine carried this one step further. In calling Americans to arms he pointed out why Americans were given this special task. Only America had dared take seriously enough the promises of God to establish the kind of society God actually intended. This opportunity must be protected at all costs because the enemies of liberty were determined to stamp out the promise America was offering humanity. Unless America preserved this freedom, it would vanish forever from the face of the world. If America could achieve her freedom, she would be the City on a Hill of inspiration and hope for all who searched for freedom.

This concept was decisive in shaping the American Creed. Out of it would come, first, the idea of the "melting pot," of America being the haven for the oppressed yearning to breathe free. Out of it, secondly, would come that distinctive American idea that since it was the first Western nation to achieve independence, the United States had the right and authority to act as custodian for the rest of the world. Out of Paine's concept, finally, would come the idea that this hard earned freedom and the attendant sacred obligation to defend life, liberty, and the pursuit of happiness were indeed the shared goals and common purpose which united and gave direction to this nation. As their ultimate rationale, the Americans, as did the Puritans earlier, found this course of action to be the will of God.

DISESTABLISHMENT

At about the same time of the War of the Revolution, the American Protestant churches were working out new forms of service and expression. The most important innovation was the virtually unanimous decision to make formal the separation of church and state. To a European this might have sounded like a contradiction: how can a nation have a common set of values and ideals given it by the Creator unless it expresses these ideals in a religious faith shared by the entire community? Had not the European experience since the Reformation proved how bloody and destructive religious pluralism could be? Would not religious rivalry constantly tear and tear and finally destroy civil society?

The reply to this came from Jefferson and Madison in their constitutional proposals, first to disestablish the Anglican church in Virginia, and then in 1787 to separate church and state in the proposed new federal constitution. This concept would become another tenet in the

American Creed. The Virginia leaders found civil leaders to be "fallible and uninspired men" just as were all other men and hence incapable of achieving any permanent monopoly on religious truth. Second, religious convictions were a matter of individual judgment, not subject to the kinds of proofs and tests of scientific evidence. Hence no human authority had the right to coerce another person into believing a religious teaching contrary to his own convictions. Finally, American experience had proved that the surest means to insure the rights of each individual was to guarantee the same rights to every other individual. If the Presbyterians, for instance, wanted religious freedom, they would have it so long as they allowed every other person to enjoy it also. Contrary to European experience, Americans had learned that religious conflict leading to violence was not inevitable, but that the best interests of all were served when the rights of all were protected.

Thus the Christian no longer needed to choose between loyalty to his church or loyalty to his nation. He was given the liberty to decide for himself whether he wanted to express any kind of loyalty to any church, without fear of civil recrimination. In the long run this sense of independence has been a great source of strength for American Protestantism. But that is our next topic of discussion.

THE VOLUNTARY PRINCIPLE

Under this new-found freedom, the American churches moved rapidly in the early 19th century toward what Sidney Mead has delineated as "the voluntary principle." [2] The churches came to conceive of themselves as voluntary associations, the products of the free and uncoerced efforts of the individual members. They found the long-standing formal disputes over theological doctrine so characteristic of European churches to be not only dull but out of harmony with their understanding of the role of the churches in America. Since God had obviously directed their activities thus far, he had still more tasks for them to fulfill in the years ahead, now that disestablishment was complete. The voluntary churches involved themselves with great energy in a wide variety of social reform programs, such as temperance, education, peace, women's rights, and above all, abolition. Only the strictly confessional churches such as the Lutheran maintained a strong emphasis on pure doctrine and high liturgical practice.

The voluntary principle limited church-related activity to those areas in which the members could agree substantially among themselves as to what they should accomplish. This virtually closed off any direct involvement by individual members in the realm of winning church-wide endorsement for political office, for creating any of the "Christian" political parties of Europe, or for a church body to work for a specific legislative proposal. Such involvement was divisive (many bodies split over abolition) and also tended to drive out members from a church who might otherwise have remained inside. With but very few exceptions, Americans came to expect their Protestant bodies to maintain this very carefully defined role within the framework of the American Creed. That consensus would persist until rudely challenged by civil rights activists in the 1960s, a story we pick up later.

MANIFEST DESTINY AND THE AMERICAN MISSION

Little has been said so far about the sorry history of race relations in the United States, a disaster which has come to haunt the discussion of American values today. In our day the questions center on: why did the white man think he could go where he wanted? to use the slave as he wanted? and still believe he was doing the will of God?

Obviously the past record of racial conflict needs no summary here.[3] What is important is to identify that complex of ideas in the 1830s and 1840s by which Americans explained to themselves and to the world why God intended that they take the land from the Indian, keep the black man in chains, and go to sleep at night with a clear conscience.

As Americans moved westward over the Appalachians, some reaching the valleys of the Pacific coast, they decided God was directly leading them. Nothing less than such a providential force could explain why they as ordinary, hardworking people, were given this cornucopia of wealth, this unspoiled Garden of Eden. That Biblical metaphor was chosen with care, because it told the pioneer what he wanted to believe: God had brought him to this place to prove to the world how durable and rewarding were the virtues of a Christian republic. They would use this untapped land to bring forth economic wealth and political liberty beyond the wildest imagination of mankind.

The settlers noted the fact that they, almost all Anglo-Saxon Protestants, were the innovators and creators in the West. They noted that the American Indian seemed interested only in subsistence living, happy to coexist with nature. They noted too that the slaves on the Southern frontier seemed capable only of menial labor and not the responsibilities of property ownership and citizenship. Thus, the white Americans concluded they had a special mission, as one editor called it, a "Manifest Destiny" to populate and develop the West for the glory of God.

This theme became incorporated into the American Dream. The pioneers came to believe that so long as they used the maximum opportunity to develop the land and resources, and so long as they remained loyal to the republican principles of the Declaration and the Constitution, they were doing the will of God. They interpreted their rugged battle for survival on the frontier as a test given them by the Almighty. God was demanding hard and persistent work, inventive ingenuity, self-discipline and patience from these pioneers just as he had from all Americans up to that time. The frontiersman recognized that test and knew God would reward those who met it bravely and directly. Thus he proudly built the roads, established the schools, founded the churches,

raised the cities, and brought government to the wilderness. On his own initiative, relying on the power of God to support him, he had conquered nature.

It was around the legend of the rugged individual pioneer that the later American hostility toward governmental welfare first developed. The argument went as follows. America was built by men willing to sacrifice and work; they had no handouts, no welfare legislation, and no guaranteed annual wage. Since they had mastered the ultimate test of their ingenuity by individual effort, they had shown future Americans what was expected of them. This theme has been one of the most durable elements in the American Creed. Even in today's television Western we see the frontier as the last unspoiled garden conquered by the personal effort of the individual American. In this manner Americans fulfilled their Manifest Destiny.[4]

"THE LAST, BEST HOPE OF EARTH"

Surely no single individual better personifies the meaning of the American Creed than Abraham Lincoln. To some a villain, to others a racist, he remains for most Americans the fulfillment of national greatness. In Lincoln the log cabin to White House myth came true. Here was the self-educated man with the best grasp of any high official on the English language. To Americans, not all of the Oxfords or aristocracies of England could produce as gifted a leader as this frontiersman.

For our purposes, Lincoln is a decisive figure because he was president during the one time American society came apart, at the juncture when the consensus over the Declaration of Independence and the mission of America no longer held her people together. As the war progressed and the casualty rolls mounted, Lincoln's own understanding of the war deepened from that of a political battle of wills into a testing of the democratic principle by the Almighty. His magisterial vision that the mission of America required it to bind up the nation's wounds closely parallels the Christian precept of forgiveness ("with malice toward none"). As did Tom Paine, Lincoln saw America as "the last, best hope of earth" for preserving liberty. To him the American Creed was a reality. It had come true for him, and he wanted to maintain its promise of opportunity for the generations to come.

From this viewpoint, Lincoln reaffirmed the goodness and providential mission of America at a time when cynicism and defeat might well have triumphed. He understood the need for the nation to reaffirm the consensus of values which had such deep meaning for him. And he moved toward reuniting the nation as painlessly as possible to get on with the business of self-government.

Lincoln's words and deeds, sometimes distorted beyond recognition by critics and by admirers, are decisive for understanding the American Creed. They reaffirm the sense of divine guidance and care which the Puritans and Jefferson had also believed, and which now were repeated in the nation's deepest crisis. Add to that the striking Biblical symbolism of Lincoln leading his people through the wilderness, to perish just at the moment of triumph, as Moses had done, and we have a benediction placed on his memory. And, it should be added, Lincoln died on Good Friday, symbolically atoning for the most foul of all deeds in the nation's history.[5] In summary, one cannot understand the meaning of Lincoln for America without understanding the religious dimension in which his career was enacted. Much of what would later be called the "civil religion" of America was, in fact, Lincoln's interpretation of the Civil War.

"THE MASTER ORGANIZERS OF THE WORLD"

After the Civil War the United States rose to pre-eminence among the industrial nations of the world. In her search for markets, products, and commercial advantage she became far more involved in world affairs than ever before in her history. The Garden of Eden had turned into the international marketplace at Jerusalem.

Obviously there were those citizens who felt this expansion was contrary to the traditional American ideals of decentralized government, agrarian individualism, and economic self sufficiency. Yet the forces of industrialization and a new aggressive patriotism soon converted most Americans to the desirability of overseas involvement. The most representative spokesmen for this new theme, which would become another tenet in the American Creed, were Theodore Roosevelt, the Rev. Josiah Strong, and Senator Albert Beveridge. In essence, theirs was but a single doctrine, one loaded with ramifications for our own day.

During the Spanish-American War of 1898 and later during his presidency, Roosevelt espoused a strong nationalist pride in American traditions. He was convinced that the United States had become wealthy and strong because she had followed God's will for fulfilling her destiny. Roosevelt concluded that with the Western frontier now settled, the United States had a God-given duty to expand overseas. She could spread Christianity, establish capitalism, and build democratic institutions for those lesser nations poor and weak. Among his many statements on this subject, one is worth quoting: "Peace is generally good in itself," but "it is only the warlike power of a civilized people that can give peace to the world."

The Rev. Josiah Strong, a highly influential leader in the missionary program of the Congregational Church, stated much the same theme. America must become a major world power because her destiny demanded it. "The Anglo-Saxon is the representative of two great ideas, which are closely related. One of them is that of civil liberty. Nearly all of the civil liberty in the world is enjoyed by Anglo-Saxons: the English, the British colonists, and the people of the United States . . ." "The other great idea . . . is that of a pure *spiritual* Christianity . . . That means that most of the spiritual Christianity in the world is found among Anglo-Saxons and their converts; for this is the great missionary race . . ." [6] He called on Anglo-Saxons to be their brother's keeper.

Senator Beveridge spelled it out in more detail. God had made the English-speaking peoples "the master organizers of the world to establish system where chaos reigns." God gave this race "the spirit of progress" to destroy forces of reaction; he made Anglo-Saxons "adept in government that we may administer government among savage and senile people . . . And of all our race He has marked the American people as His chosen nation to finally lead in the regeneration of the world. This is the divine mission of America . . . Where dwells the fear of God, the American people move forward to the future of their hope and the doing of His work . . ." [7]

Some readers may charge all this off as political rhetoric. Perhaps that is true, but coming at a time of unparalleled American economic expansion, these ideas greatly strengthened the convictions of those citizens who were keeping alive their sense of mission, not only at home but throughout the world.

THE WAR TO END ALL WARS

In the administration of President Woodrow Wilson (1913-1921), something of the older Calvinist tradition reappeared as the basis for American domestic and foreign policies. It is the latter which concerns us here, especially the terms by which Wilson justified American participation in World War I. This feat would contribute another tenet to the American Creed—that the United States is not only the carrier of Christianity and capitalism to the world, but is now quite literally the savior of that world against the forces of oppression and death.

A devout Presbyterian, Wilson perhaps more than any other president sought consciously to infuse specific Christian ethical teachings into his public leadership. This was his Calvinist heritage: the belief that a precise Christian position on the major issues could be determined. In 1911, for instance, on the 300th "birthday" of the King James Version of the Bible, he said that "America was born a Christian nation to exemplify that devotion to the elements of righteousness which are derived from

35

the revelations of Holy Scripture." In 1914 he stated Americans were "custodians of the spirit of righteousness, of the spirit of equal-handed justice, of the spirit of hope."

This vision helps to explain his course of action when America faced the question of whether to enter World War I. Her own shores had not been invaded; thus no immediate threat to her domestic security existed. Yet the United States did go to war because, in Wilson's words, civilization itself was "seeming to be in the balance." The time had come "when America is privileged to spend her blood and might for the principles that gave her birth, and happiness and peace which she has treasured."

During the war and the peace treaty negotiations, Wilson won tremendous support from the Allies for the general principles he put forward. For instance, he insisted this would be "a war to end all wars," "a war to make the world safe for democracy," "a peace without victory." So sure was Wilson that democracy harmonized with the will of God that he believed once its principles were enacted around the world, the threat of future wars would be destroyed. Most important for us was the fact that Wilson cast the United States in the role of leader for this new world of peace. As did Jefferson, Lincoln, and so many others, Wilson believed that the internal stability, the economic wealth and the resourceful populace of America were proof that God indeed expected great things of that nation now that she was a mature member of the world. In fact, God was demanding that America assert the truth of her mission by rescuing the world from the disasters created during the war.

Americans really believed Wilson in 1917 as he asked for the declaration of war. The Americans made the sacrifices, sent the young men, paid the taxes, and they hailed the victory as final proof of the righteousness of their goals. If the high hopes for peace without victory failed to materialize in the 1920s, the blame was not to rest on America, since her work was the work of God.

"THE CHAMPIONS OF TOLERANCE, AND DECENCY, AND FREEDOM, AND FAITH"

As we know too well, Wilson's lofty vision for world peace and international government never materialized. Other forces were at work in Europe and Asia, leading the people of several nations to follow the darkened vision of dictatorship. This time, as all but England fell before the blitzkrieg of the Nazis, the American people had a far more visible and identifiably evil enemy standing as a mortal threat to their fundamental values. President Franklin D. Roosevelt did not need to cast the role of American participation into World War II into the same idealistic terms used by President Wilson. The diabolical nature of Naziism and the attack on Pearl Harbor accomplished that task.

For our purposes, what is significant is that once again the United States accepted the role of the savior of the world. President Roosevelt called on the populace early in 1942 to preserve "tolerance, and decency, and freedom, and faith." Most Americans understood the war as something close to a holy crusade in which the stakes really were the survival of Christianity and freedom. They believed this was no war merely of technological skill or of military tactics; this was a testing of the very soul of America. Perhaps more than at any other time in her history, the American people were solidly united in a common purpose.

The outcome of World War II solidified the American Creed. The U.S. victory was nothing less than the will of God. This victory redeemed the fantastic loss of life, the hardships of mobilization, the increase in taxes, and everything else which Americans had invested in winning the war. And this victory explains why many of those over thirty are so fervid in their pride in America's accomplishments.

Let us here briefly summarize the shaping of the American Creed. From the Puritans to Franklin D. Roosevelt, Americans have been absorbing this creed into their sense of nationality.[8] The City on a Hill; the Creator's

37

bestowal of life, liberty and the pursuit of happiness; the Puritan ethic; the voluntary principle; Manifest Destiny; America as the last, best hope; the Anglo-Saxon's responsibility; and America as savior of the world—these themes are the landmark expressions of those intangible but deeply felt goals and common purposes which have kept the nation united, with but one exception, for nearly two hundred years.

They have served America this long because, perhaps, for many millions of citizens these goals seemed to come true in their own lifetimes. This was not true for the racial minorities, to be sure. But for the majority of people the vision of America as the land of opportunity for mankind was real. A second factor helping to explain the long-standing loyalty of Americans to these themes is the topic of our next chapter, the ritualization of the American Dream.

THE
RITES
OF
PATRIOTISM

3

Until our day most Americans have acknowledged the need for ritualistic expression of loyalty to the nation. Little serious objection has been raised to the manner in which a viable consensus between the government and the church bodies over religious influences in government and religious observances has been conducted. No one, for instance, is calling for the repeal of Memorial Day or for abolishing Thanksgiving. Christmas is still a legal holiday. Governmental officials in their official capacity attend funerals of important public leaders conducted in church buildings with a large display of patriotic and military ritual. The American flag is lowered in respect for dead leaders during the church funeral. In these and other ways Americans have developed a visible set of rites and symbols reflecting their religious understanding of loyalty based on their dedication to the American Creed.

This chapter probes the extent to which the current crisis—dissent, the resistance to the draft, the flag controversy—are the results of the nation's dividing loyalty over the need for such ritual and symbol. The issues, however, go even deeper than that. Americans are divided because they seem no longer able to agree on the need for agreement! Perhaps if we back up and take a long view of the basic issues concerning the religious expression of loyalty and patriotism, we can better understand the disputes today.

WHAT IS LOYALTY?

We should first ask, To what are men loyal and for what reasons? A helpful starting point is an excellent study by Morton Grodzins, *The Loyal and the Disloyal: Social Boundaries of Patriotism and Treason*.[1] He first points out that loyalty is created by social forces; it is not inherent in human nature. Loyalty develops out of a sense of need. Man needs society for protection, for economic opportunity, and for social intercourse. Man identifies with specific groups and ideals reflected by the group. These ideals are the result of a common language, a common history, geographical cohesion, religious consensus, or a combination of any of these.

From this identification man learns the needs for and the rewards of loyalty to the group or to the nation. Without loyalties he could not organize his existence; he would have no sense of stability or direction for his social life. Man would be faced with the never-ending dilemma of having to provide for *all* his basic needs— self defense, fire and crime prevention, and the like— besides tending to his occupation and his family. Without a minimal loyalty, Grodzins concludes, men would lapse into "wild and random inconsistencies or into a brooding state of confusion and indecisiveness . . ."[2]

The means by which loyalty to the state has been achieved have not been uniformly peaceful or voluntary.

Especially in the 20th century in the Atlantic community of nations, the all-powerful military state has used direct coercion, rather than appeal to common loyalty, to achieve stability. Once in power these superstates made skillful use of mass propaganda programs to promote national unity. So successful have some of these become that loyalty to the government as the only agency of salvation has turned into religious worship.[3]

By voluntary or forceful means, the nation-state of our day knows it remains in power so long as it furnishes its citizenry with programs and ideals with which they can identify, that is, which give meaning to their public life. Whether they take the form of public education of children, or protection of freedom of religion, or some economic security program, the means by which the state shows its concern for the populace are understood as evidence of mutual respect. So long as the state maintains that sense of concern, the citizenry displays its loyalty, or at least refrains from disloyal acts.[4]

But when the state acts contrary to this sense of identification, the citizenry calls for change. Usually this call starts quietly, then increases in intensity when little or no reform is made. Finally, if all non-violent means of change seem to be closed to the dissidents, they may resort to physical force through revolution or comparable direct action.

THE NEED FOR RITUAL

Almost all national states have consciously attempted to prevent such dislocation before it begins. Historically this has been achieved most frequently by deliberately encouraging citizens to involve themselves in patriotic rituals and ceremonies celebrating the virtues and glories of the nation. At times, as in Nazi Germany, such rituals were contrived. At other times, such expression of patriotism emerged without official encouragement or promotion. In any case, every nation celebrates itself with a wide variety of symbolic rituals serving to remind the populace of its common heritage and destiny.

With our understanding of the American Creed, we can perceive now why we take patriotic rites and symbols very seriously. Symbols are recognized as visual substitutes for all of the shared values and ideals of this nation.

Some illustrations here will be helpful. American patriotic lore has its sacred shrines: the Tomb of the Unknown Soldier, the tombs of Grant and Lee, Independence Hall, and the Capitol in Washington, D. C. These are patriotic versions of temples of worship or shrines in which loyalty to the higher cause is expressed. One finds the same at Westminster Abbey in London or the Arch of Triumph in Paris or the Victor Emmanuel monument in Rome. Within the patriotic shrines one finds objects which serve the same functions as holy objects within temples. There are statutes of the great leaders, as there are of the saints. There are photographs, or furniture, or clothing used by the national leaders.

In comparable fashion, the nation celebrates certain holidays as the churches celebrate holy days. Carlton J. H. Hayes points to the similarities between the Fourth of July and Christmas (both are birthdays); or Flag Day and Corpus Christi Day; or Veterans' Day and All Saints' Day. Similarly the birthdays of Lincoln and Washington receive special commemorative attention.[5]

The closest parallel of all, of course, is Memorial Day. Lloyd Warner presents an extended analysis of the rites of that day.[6] Memorial Day confronts the participants with vivid symbols of life and death, since the ceremonies are held in cemeteries. But the day's rites offer those in attendance an explanation of the death they see symbolized around them. Death is overcome, and the unity and purpose of the nation is reaffirmed by a conscious invocation of past traditions which have served the people in time of war. The deaths of the soldiers are redeemed by the triumph of the higher cause of the nation. The tragedy of the loss of life is overcome by the understanding that such sacrifice was the supreme expression of loyalty. Beyond that, Memorial Day has always been transdenominational. Catholics, Jews, and Protestants could observe it together with no fears of compromising their convictions. Again a national rite serves to unify the people around a common set of symbols.

In like manner, Americans in our day created a comparable religious ceremony with strong patriotic overtones at the funeral for Senator Robert F. Kennedy. Although the Roman Catholic funeral mass with its accent on hope, resurrection, and heavenly life were very evident, this was a ritual transcending sectarian loyalties. Senator Kennedy's death was interpreted as an event with meaning and purpose because he had given his own life in service to others. The preacher at the funeral outlined the senator's deams for minorities, and his vision for America as becoming again the land of opportunity for all. The minister said, "Especially in this hour, we must keep faith with America and her destiny and we must not forsake our trust in one another."[7] Here again the American people came together in a common purpose centered on common ideals and aspirations, and they invoked the Christian faith in their rededication to national goals.

Several factors help to account for the durability of these rites. In the United States this kind of observance is easier to perpetuate, because in most instances the American government does not coerce direct public participation. No one has to fly the flag, or march on Memorial Day or give thanks on Thanksgiving, or visit Arlington National Cemetery. Such observances are voluntary, and therefore easier to maintain over a long period.

Furthermore, and this is decisive for our study, several tenets in the American Creed bear directly on the issue of patriotic rites. Almost all of these rituals are religious in meaning, reflecting again the American conviction of the chosen people, the nation with a sacred mission. That being the case, its people accept the responsibility of expressing this sense of mission in appropriate form— that is, by a form of religious worship and celebration.

One can add the voluntary principle here as another support for patriotic rites. Those who participate believe their patriotism is stronger because it is voluntarily given. To sum up, those Americans for whom patriotic ceremonies are meaningful are able to reconcile their loyalty to God with that of loyalty to the nation. They see no necessary conflict between the two loyalties because they believe that so long as the United States follows the will of God in her national policies, she follows a course of action worthy of the honor which the rites express.

SIGNS AND SYMBOLS

The relationship between religious and patriotic sentiment is expressed in many other ways. Every session of Congress, and of most state legislatures, opens with prayer by an officially designated chaplain. The "Eye of Providence" is on the dollar bill. The national motto, "In God We Trust" is stamped on national coins. In the 1950s the phrase "under God" was added to the Pledge of Allegiance, in itself an act very close to a religious commitment, such as confirmation.

One finds many parallels in national hymns and in sacred songs. What child does not learn "America the Beautiful" or "America" or "The Battle Hymn of the Republic"? The latter is something of an authentic folk hymn in American culture. It broke out spontaneously among the mourners at the many depots through which Senator Kennedy's funeral train travelled, as it did during the memorial service for him at the 1968 Democratic National Convention. The parallels between the assassinated Lincoln and the assassinated Kennedys have reached deeply into American patriotic ritual.

A little known but superb example serving to summarize this discussion is found in a book, *The Faith of America: Readings, Songs and Prayers for the Celebration of American Holidays*, published in 1963 by the Reconstructionist Press, New York. In the Introduction, the editors point out that the programs are interfaith in nature, and lend a "religious interpretation to American history and institutions without reference to the specific doctrines or any of the historic religions" of Americans. Again, the conscious effort is to find the common ground on which the many groups calling themselves Americans can meet. The programs of readings, songs, poetry, and Scripture are intended to be used on New Year's Day, Lincoln's Birthday, Washington's Birthday, Memorial Day, Flag Day, Independence Day, Labor Day, Constitution Day, Columbus Day, United Nations Day, Election Day, and Thanksgiving Day.

Lest any reader conclude that our discussion thus far is basically critical of the patriotic-religious dimension, let it be said here that our purpose is to summarize what does exist and what is exceedingly important for a large number of Americans. The final chapter will show how, on the basis of devotion to the American Creed and these rites, the great crises of our day are the results of conflicting understandings of the extent to which Americans owe loyalty to these traditions.[8]

WHAT CAUSED THE LOYALTY CRISIS?

4

Why the bumper stickers? Where did things start going wrong in the United States? Where did that vision which burned so brightly during World War II regarding a just and lasting peace start to turn dim?

It seems that the United States started redividing actually during the war and shortly thereafter. The war had produced tremendous changes within the nation itself—in the millions of citizens mobilized, the huge numbers of civilians who moved to war industry cities, and in the sharp rise in the standard of living for many.

THE COLD WAR

More directly, however, the shape of post-war America was created by the sudden antagonism in relations between the Soviet Union and the United States. As the

Russians unfolded their plans after 1945 for maintaining control of the East European nations and for encouraging world communism, Americans turned bitter, and then enraged over what they believed was Russia's betrayal of the terms of peace in 1945.

Americans had understood that all the Allies wanted was what Woodrow Wilson had wanted two decades earlier: no more war, elimination of colonialism, open diplomacy, a world tribunal for peacekeeping, and self-determination for the small nations. They thought the aim of the war was to preserve the "Four Freedoms": from fear and want, and freedom of speech and of religion.

Now Americans were told the Communists were destroying these aims and freedoms by adding small countries and colonies to their worldwide empire. Having cast itself in the role of peacekeeper, the United States now found itself for the first time on the defensive. Something was wrong; something very serious had interfered with the original goals that had given this nation the strength and willpower it needed to win the war. It could not be that the American Creed was in error; God would not have allowed that to happen. The only conclusion, for many, was that somewhere within this nation itself some powerful leaders no longer believed in the mission of their country.

Gradually in the late 1940s there appeared the "internal conspiracy" interpretation of America's failure to resist Russian expansion. This thesis, advanced by well-meaning citizens and by political office seekers, pinned the blame of American diplomacy on those within the nation who had "sold out to Communism." Rather than keep up pride in individual enterprise, the indictment read, these Americans were bringing in the welfare state. Rather than keep the government close to the people, these "traitors" were turning their future over to the planned tinkerings of bureaucrats. Rather than take the initiative abroad, the charges continued, the soft-headed American leaders were afraid to take preventive action against the Reds. In this manner, went the conclusion, the United States was being defeated from within. No Soviet soldier would have to die as long as the United States kept slipping down that well-greased path from liberalism to socialism, and then into Communism.[1]

This "conspiracy" interpretation caught on among large numbers of Americans in the early 1950s. From its perspective they could now fit everything in place. Those who seemed only politically liberal before were now undoubtedly giving aid and comfort to the enemy. Those who ignored or scoffed at formal patriotic ceremonies were making the Kremlin leaders very happy. Those clergy who preached the "brotherhood of man" instead of old-time gospel were actually agents of the one-world delusion. So the indictment read.

What is significant for our purposes is that the nation became bitterly divided over the issue of loyalty to the nation. This was a most complex issue because it was so deeply infused with charges of treason, subversion, and betrayal of American values. Those suspicions were not easily reconciled by the more familiar processes of open discussion and constructive criticism. Once a prominent citizen had been accused of being "soft on Communism" or being "anti-American," he found himself faced with a kind of resistance which would not be erased by reason or evidence.

The antidote suggested by the supporters of the internal conspiracy thesis was a huge dosage of "old-fashioned Americanism" as defined in 1954 by Billy Graham. Unquestionably he spoke for millions of citizens when he proposed a five-point counterattack against those within the nation he felt were disloyal: (1) a return to earlier expressions of Americanism, those ideals which led Americans to build "the greatest nation ever to exist in all history"; (2) a return to conservative, evangelical Christianity by which he meant a personal faith in God, accepting the Bible as the norm for faith and ethics, and a conversion experience; (3) a return to prayer; (4) an authentic religious revival by which, Graham pointed out, the nation would be rid of "the rats and termites that are subversively endeavoring to weaken the defense of this nation from within"; and (5) personal Christian witnessing. In other words, Graham called on Americans to assume their responsibilities as carriers of God's sacred mission. That goal had made the United States the world's savior once; that goal was still within the reach of the populace now.[2]

THE VOICE OF THE EXTREMIST

During the late 1950s, however, the issue of Communist subversion faded from immediate public concern. The Soviets did not launch a nuclear war; their visible split with Communist China weakened American fears of a monolithic Communist plot; and the all-American patriots could not find a charismatic leader among them to keep the fires brightly burning. Beyond that, some of the extremely right-wing public patriots, best exemplified by the John Birch Society, claimed the mantle of leadership among the God-loves-America-best citizenry. Their conclusions, especially those of Robert Welch, were simply not believed by the great majority of Americans. Such staunch conservatives as Senator Barry Goldwater and editor William F. Buckley, Jr., rejected the Birchers when they claimed President Eisenhower was a dedicated agent of the Communist conspiracy. Almost all other conservatives did the same.

Yet the far rightists had an impact far beyond their limited numbers. The Birchers and the other self-appointed crusaders were able to heat up the rhetoric of loyalty and patriotism in the 1960s, much as had been done a decade earlier over suspected traitors in government. Now, however in the early '60s, the far right broadened the definition of disloyalty far beyond that of the earlier era. In accepting the internal conspiracy thesis, they found treason not only in the government, but in every phase of American life. Disloyalty, they announced to the nation, was rampant in certain Sunday school curricula, the League of Women Voters, the Girl Scouts, Wheaton College, the Billy Graham Crusade, and the Old Fashioned Revival Hour—to name some of the institutions which had not been on the lists of alleged un-American activities before.[3] Obviously the far right had no visible success in winning converts to this bill of goods. But it did keep in front of the public the highly emotional issue of loyalty and patriotism.

As the first serious signs of dissent over the war, the draft, and campus life started to appear in the mid '60s, the far right quickly absorbed the new wave of protest into its conspiracy interpretation. It claimed that everything from race riots to demonstrating clergymen, from welfare demonstrators to draft dodgers, was more evidence of the new anti-Americanism abroad in the land. Bumper stickers started to appear.

THE REPLY FROM THE LEFT

Without any specific shape or form, a rebellion against this interpretation of loyalty came out of the left wing in American political life in the mid 1960s. This faction shared the far rightist fears of a rapidly declining America. But they put the blame squarely on the heads of the right wing heroes—the military-industrial leaders who to the leftist were leading America directly into a fascist police state. Their aim, the leftists argued, was to reduce the people to servitude by giving them economic security, to quiet dissent in the name of law and order, to crush authentic peoples' uprisings around the world in the name of anti-communism, and then when their program was complete, to sit back and feast on the wealth and power they had created.

The left wing also called for a return to old fashioned American idealism. The rapid and widespread surge of far left opinion in this decade was the final element needed to bring on the great social crises of our own day. With this background in mind, we move into the specific issues themselves.

TWO VIEWS OF LOYALTY: REVOLUTIONIST AND TRADITIONALIST

5

A brief note here will explain the format and choice of subjects. We will examine public welfare and racism, minority and student dissent, the draft, activist clergy, the use of the flag, and the Pentagon papers. These obviously represent only some of the critical issues of the day. They are selected for discussion for two reasons. Each is of immediate concern to us and will not go away if ignored. Second, each question constitutes a clear expression of the general problem of loyalty. Questions such as pollution are real enough, but are not disputed in the manner in which the topics of this study are examined.

It seems fair also to raise the question here: is not part of our problem that the United States may have promised too much? Is it possible that the ideals expressed in the

American Creed are so lofty and noble as to be, in fact, unattainable and thus causing the cynicism of our day? I suggest this dilemma as a focus point from which to study the issues raised below. Americans expect peace, economic security, justice, and opportunity. One does not find similar expectations in most of the rest of the world. Thus the dilemma of the gap between promise and reality.

In our day, however, we are not content to let it go as being simply a "dilemma." This is the age of activism, of achievement, of standing up to be counted. And when we find our problems increasing rather than declining, we want scapegoats. The right wing blames the left and vice versa. The wealthy and the poor blame each other; the generations find monumental gaps preventing any understanding. Patriot and dissenter blame the evils of American life on his particular adversary. Bumper stickers close off further analysis.

These comments are not to suggest that simply by more dialog these problems would necessarily fade away. It is to suggest that we must recognize that the United States has promised her people more personal fulfillment than any other nation in history, and that her people want immediate delivery.

One final note — this on organization. Both to vary the pace of the text and to make the material as life-like as possible, I have restructured the narrative into a different format. For each issue I have (1) described the question at stake in terms of the conflict over loyalty to the American Creed; (2) presented the more far reaching interpretations of the issues in the form of a give and take exchange of views between "Traditionalist" and "Revolutionist"; and (3) summarized the issue in the form of discussion questions. The purpose is to help the reader reach decisions on these issues.

WELFARE, THE GHETTO, AND THE PURITAN ETHIC

This issue obviously is deeply intertwined with that of poverty, job and educational discrimination, and automation. This makes a constructive solution to the problem under discussion that much more difficult. But, for purposes of discussion, we can describe the issue:

> To what extent is the mushrooming number of welfare recipients, especially minority ghetto dwellers, a rejection of the traditional American ideal of the Puritan ethic? Is one solution within the framework of loyalty to the United States found with the encouragement of ethnic self-determination programs?

Dialog

REVOLUTIONIST: No one on welfare really wants to be there; let's get that straight. We didn't ask to be born poor and stuffed into overcrowded schools with underpaid teachers and worn-out equipment. If the United States prides herself so much on "education for citizenship," why doesn't she make a real effort to clean up the ghetto schools? Give the kids a trade; give them some pride in themselves, and don't just pen them up in a box until they are 16 and then turn them loose for unemployment checks. It's a vicious circle: we're poor because we can't get an education because we're black because whitey wants to keep it that way.

If you think we have it so good on welfare, come down and try it yourself. One of your establishment people did, the food editor of the *New York Times*. He reported "irritability, great tedium, and difficulty in preparing adequate meals, and constant hunger." The money we get doesn't even pay for our food, so that means there is nothing for soap, napkins, toothpaste, or a telephone. Try living on 25 dollars a week with two kids and see how good it is.

We know as well as you that welfare is just treating the symptoms, not the causes. It is strictly patch-up work for the kind of world we live in. Did we build the rotten tenements we live in? Do we have any control over our own lives, like our own schools? Are we the ones who let the landlords get by without giving us our legal

55

services? Some things stink here but *we* didn't make it that way.

TRADITIONALIST: Hold on now, let's get this straight. You don't work; you don't pay taxes; you don't keep up your property; you have as many kids as you want and unload them on the streets; you get socialized this and welfare that; and it's all free, and you're complaining? Guess who pays for your free load? It's me and all the other straights like me. We have to work hard, pay our taxes, obey the law, take pride in our neighborhood, so you can live without working. Some deal! Don't give me any of this "I can't help it" stuff. This is a free country, and anyone who wants to work can get a job. Sure, he might not get his first choice; sure, he might have to work nights. But he is making his own way without a handout or a "gimme" attitude. The only reason we can support so many freeloaders on welfare is because there are so many in this country who are willing to work hard, who do take pride in their own efforts, and who do pay their bills without expecting a free ride.

That's the trouble with America today: the old pioneer spirit is gone. Who would settle out in the wilderness today, clearing the land, building the house, planting the crops, starting the schools and churches, *and* be happy to do it? They weren't rich, but they had pride, and you can't get that in your unemployment check. Sure, some people get bad breaks; I know of a mother with ten children where the father just up and left, and they can't find him. She needs help and we should pitch in. But not forever, and let's blow the whistle right now on this idea that the welfare people are entitled to money. No one is entitled to anything free in this life.

You know what the real trouble is with most of you: you're just lazy. You're like the drones in the beehive waiting for the workers to bring back the goodies so you can cut in on your share. Some people are like that; it must be in their heredity. But this country would never be as great as it is, unless its people really went to work and built it up from nothing. And take a look at what the United States has done for the world, not just for herself. She stopped the Nazis cold, she gave the world those wonder drugs and medicines, and all that Marshall Plan aid, and Point Four, and the relief during disasters, and those agricultural discoveries. Good old fashioned American know-how! And when those foreigners spat in our face, we kept on giving. That's what makes America great, not those drones.

REVOLUTIONIST: Big deal! We've heard that speech so many times we know it by heart. Believe it or not, many of those on relief and welfare just cannot get off the rolls, especially if they're not lily-white educated middle class. Whitey keeps talking about life, liberty, and the pursuit of happiness, and about America being the land of opportunity. But he is talking about *his* kind of country, not ours. He made this country for himself, and let us shine his shoes or carry his luggage. Take your Thomas Jefferson and his Declaration. He was also the biggest racist you could imagine. Let me quote from the record: "I advance it therefore as a suspicion only, that the blacks, whether originally a distinct race, or made distinct by time and circumstance, are inferior to the whites in the endowments both of body and mind." Some author of liberty! And your churches, with their brotherhood of man. Until we started marching and raising hell, you know the most segregated hour of the week in America was church time, Sunday a.m. You didn't give us a chance.

O.K. You want some facts. In America the way to get ahead is to work, stick to your job, use your brain, put your savings to work, keep up on the law and order. Fine. But the record shows blacks and the other minorities cannot get credit. Most blacks have to be salaried instead of self-employed because whitey won't trust them with a loan. And since the black man never had much collateral to start with, he isn't considered a very good risk. Besides that, the white man raises our insurance rates far above yours, and you know why. He thinks blacks just love to riot and burn down buildings or let them run down. And prices; that's another case. We can prove that supermarket food prices are higher in our neighborhoods than in the superswell suburbs. So, think about that: rents, loan rates, insurance, food costs all are higher in the ghetto. And you say we enjoy living here!

Let's get at some more facts. Let's talk about getting a job so we can get off the rolls. Look at those who learned a trade, passed the tests, and then looked for work. You know there aren't very many integrated unions. In St. Louis, in the mid '60s out of 1,667 apprentices in on-the-job training, seven were black. In Atlanta 20 out of 700 construction apprentice workers were black, and they got the dirty jobs like plastering and cement finishing. In Baltimore the record was 20 black apprentices out of 750 on the job. In Detroit less than two percent of all craft union apprentices were black.

So what did we do about it? We developed black pride in black capitalism, black communities, and black self-help. We know we aren't welcome out there in the suburbs or the country clubs or the churches. OK, let it be. But we want the right to take care of ourselves. If that means keeping whitey out of our part of town, that's the way it will be. We want full local self-determination of our lives and our institutions. We want to run our own schools. What do white teachers know about the problems of a black youngster? How can they understand what it takes to be ready for integration?

We know what's best for our children, and we don't want any labor union or Ford Foundation or downtown schoolboard telling us that if we want their money we have to do things their way. We are doing things our way: our curriculum, our teachers, our standards. You do the same for your children. Fair is fair, isn't that the American way? Government, of, by, and for the people; that's what black power is all about, and this time the government is for us.

Don't you see what the white man has done? He has made the minorities live in his colonies just as if we were some wild tribe in Africa or the South Pacific. He tells us what we can and can't do; he tells us we have to fight his wars, pay his taxes, pass his union tests, obey his laws. And what for? So we can live just like him. He doesn't want us living together in our own culture. He still thinks America is the land of the "melting pot" where everything is boiled into one big stew. Well, blackness can't be melted.

TRADITIONALIST. I'll buy most of that. The blacks were treated worse than we can ever imagine. And I know we can't go back to the old clichés like "look at George Washington Carver or Jackie Robinson" anymore. That day has long passed.

But let me make just one point here. How can the black child ever get out of the cycle of poverty, segregation, inferior education, and the rest if he is isolated from the rest of America? Sure, the ghettos are colonies; yes, the white man exploits him with loans, credit, and the rest. But black pride leading to complete black control over the schools, and churches and businesses in black areas only makes those areas even worse colonies than they are now.

Our schools aren't perfect. Maybe some of those union teachers are thinking more of protecting their own jobs than they are about the students when they strike the black schools, or refuse to let black people run the schools. But that doesn't mean we have to go all the way in the other direction. Let's keep revising our textbooks. We did get rid of that all-white Dick-Jane-Spot reader. We got rid of Little Black Sambo. All kinds of ethnic folk music is being taught youngsters. That's a small start, but it is a start.

And money. If you won't take the white man's money, will you really be able to get enough of your own in your school district to give the kids the kind of intensive education they need? They need lots of specialists: remedial reading specialists, counselors, well-trained social studies teachers, the complete works. So I say, keep talking with the foundation money men. They've come a long way already, and they want to help. No one in America has complete self-control over all the institutions of his community. That's the price you pay for living in the 20th century.

No one is asking you to start waving the red, white, and blue; no one is asking you to accept the Founding Fathers as your founding fathers. But once you choose to live in America, you choose to live by the rules America sets up for all of us. You want to change them? Go right ahead, but until they are changed, they are the rules. If you don't like them, no one is stopping you from leaving.

We have to work these things out as best we can together, in community, and not retreat into our own corners. That's what I am afraid is happening. Black power, chicano power, red power—why can't we get back to people power? America is still the land where people come first.

Discussion Questions

1. If everyone is agreed on the need for drastic reform of welfare programs, why is progress so hard to achieve?

2. Can reform of welfare ever take place so long as we hold to the Puritan Ethic?

3. To what extent have the following developments forced us to rethink our earlier loyalty to the Puritan Ethic? Overproduction, leisure time, automation, longer life span, social security, and the union shop.

4. Would private charity—such as the foundations and the churches—be willing or able to take up the slack if the federal government got out of welfare?

5. Is the United States still the land of opportunity for individual initiative and the pioneer spirit? Are those who stay on welfare acting in an un-American manner?

6. Is black power, or chicano, or red power, a threat to national unity and the need for shared ideals? Would

our society come apart if these movements were allowed to grow without controls?

7. Would national unity and maximum educational opportunity for all be sacrificed if total local control over education is enacted?

8. Should the ethnic minorities develop their own recognized symbols and rituals of loyalty?

STUDENT DISSENT

Is the turmoil on the campuses an expression of honest youthful idealism hoping to build a better America? Or is it a failure of the students to understand the need for disciplined effort to make the best use of their opportunities? Are the means employed consistent with the means Americans have used to bring about needed reforms in society?

Dialog

REVOLUTIONIST: What we want on campus is simple; we want to get back to the fundamentals. We want to learn how to save ourselves and the world. It really comes down to that. We want to relate to each other, to get rid of all our hangups and hypocrisy. We haven't done this before, you know. We have been so tied up in materialistic and security goals that we have forgotten what real education is all about; we want self knowledge.

To achieve this, we have to take bold, even revolutionary action. Look at the mess all around us. Look at the war, the pollution, the racism, the poverty, the phoniness we find. Is that what our educational system is geared to produce? If it is, then we want no part of it. We don't want to learn how to kill one another or cheat or oppress one another. We want to learn how to love and share with everyone. Let the love come in; it's there if we would let it.

All these subjects and grades and papers and requirements are so much control by the establishment to keep us in our place. They want to brainwash us so we can turn out as carbon copies of those in command now. It only proves how afraid people really are of becoming themselves. We want to change all that, we want to tear down the artificial barriers and the regimentation, the bureaucracy, and the IBM cards and the rules. We want to establish authentic community where people relate freely and control their own lives.

But the power structure doesn't want this. It has too much money invested, and too much prestige to let anything so radical take charge on campus. So we are kept in line. We don't have any real control over our lives. Isn't America supposed to be a land of individual choice and self-determination? A land where people have the right to be left alone by the government, the church, or anyone else? Well then, let's give that right to young adults as well as to older ones. Let's let them decide for themselves who their roommates should be, what kind of work should be expected for a college degree, what kind of teachers and administrators we want. Let's get real community, like our brothers in the ghetto are establishing.

TRADITIONALIST: You call that an education? You talk about living up to American ideals about individualism. Nowhere in the American past can you find the schools offering the kind of romantic mush you want. The United States became great because her people were willing to put their minds as well as their bodies to work. Medicine, engineering, law, technology, business: these were the occupations which attracted the best minds and offered the rewards of life. And students didn't sit around mooning over each other's hangups and bruised egos.

Education is for self-improvement, which in turn serves society. Everyone wants "community"; no one is talking about going back to cave dwelling. But community is not created just by talking about it or brooding over it, or by thinking no one in this country has ever tried to solve these problems before you did. Why should you know enough about the outside world to know what courses you will need? With the high costs of education, why should parents be expected to keep you searching for community instead of learning civil engineering?

This desire for self-determination without self-discipline is really anti-American—I mean that just the way you heard it. It is thumbing your nose at American pride in its achievements, in its ability to provide more food, medicine, and technical know-how to the underdeveloped nations of the world. Where would we be today if we hadn't provided career education? Back in the Stone Age hunting jackrabbits with slingshots.

Everyone in America is expected to make his contribution to the nation as well as receive its benefits. You students don't know how good you've got it. You can come and go as you please—loaf, dabble, vacation, and still get the kind of education that most young people in the world would go into debt for for the rest of their lives. How do you expect to solve the problems of pollution, racism, war, and poverty by soul-searching? The real American tradition is problem solving. Instead of sitting around expecting you have the right to four free years of education, free sex, and free whatnot, you should be preparing yourselves for some real problem solving.

Who has done more for the underdogs and the oppressed in this world than some men with solid education? Martin Luther King had an earned doctorate, Ralph Nader is a trained attorney, Norman Borlaug has his Ph.D., not to mention all those M.D.'s who have given the world those fantastic vaccines. They didn't sit around feeling oppressed or exploited. They went out and achieved. Nobody is stopping you from doing the same.

Yes, I agree with you; let's get back to fundamentals. What does this have to do with loyalty? Everything, I think, because you show loyalty to what you think is the most important thing in life. If your religion and your feeling for your country leads you to want to help others, then your loyalty to that should lead you to make the best use of your opportunities. When you do that, you serve yourself, your country, and your faith. Isn't that what it's all about?

REVOLUTIONIST: But that's just what we are trying to do on campus—make our studies relevant to life. We want to get involved, to help bring to the world all those good things you told us were our inalienable right, like life, liberty, and happiness. That *is* what it's all about. But what have you done? You say America is the land of promise and opportunity and mission. But what do we find: militarism, pollution, hypocrisy, the double standard for races, materialistic goals, curtailment of freedom. What kind of wonderful world is that you're giving us? After all, we are the future and we want to determine the direction it will go. That's why we want to get involved in planning our studies and our lives and our morals. It's our life, not yours. So, let's get back to the purpose of education: making better people out of us. What's so outdated about love, brotherhood, peace, and freedom? What's so bad about giving the power back to the students—to the people?

TRADITIONALIST: I'll tell you what is so bad about that. The ideals are fine, no argument there. But you cast everything in terms of either/or. You are the pure idealists who are going to save the world without doing anything more than marching and rioting and talking about it. Your self-righteousness really turns off most of us who have had some experience in the college of hard knocks.

What would happen, for instance, if we had another depression and your parents took away all that money? Would you be willing to dig ditches? A lot of successful men today did just that in the '30s. Or what if the United States got into a really serious war? Would you be willing to defend her? We did; we lived through a depression and a war and we know the options in life aren't just yes or no. No one is so perfect that he can save mankind.

So, you say you want to save America because you believe in her ideals. Well, this is a democracy and you have to get along with others; you have to respect the rights and the power of the majority. You are learning that the majority isn't so all fired hot about your pure idealism. Some even think that most college kids are spoiled punks who need a good swift kick in the pants. They have the votes, remember, and they want to keep it that way. Those who want to get into political office are going to have to please the majority as well as pleasing you. So that's why there is so much resentment towards the campuses today; the students don't know how good they've got it.

Put it this way. Why do you feel the world *has* to go the way you want it to? Why are you talking at the ripe old age of 19 of being "sick and tired" with our government? Sick and tired? You ought to live where you can't complain out loud.

You say you want freedom, you tell us the freedom revolution is here. OK. Let's look at that for a moment. Just by proclaiming the revolution is here doesn't mean that it is. What have you really done to convert the average wage earner, the hard hats, to your revolution? You sneer at what they hold sacred; you waste the opportunities they can't have; you act as though freedom means doing anything you want to do.

That reminds me of another "revolution," the one in France in 1792. They were so all fired sure theirs was the New Age for mankind they even started numbering the calendar over again, starting with the year One. They had their sloppy clothes and long hair, everyone calling each other "citizen" or "brother." And look what happened. All their revolution got them was a lot of mass murders and finally a military strong man who put law and order back into the country again. So every country needs stability as well as liberty, but it seems every generation has to learn that for itself.

But let's be more specific. What is wrong with "power to the people"? How would it work? How would it really control pollution, for example? What if every town along a river had different standards of water purity or air purity or whatever? How would you stop one city from polluting the water of another? Or how would you protect yourself against crime, when all it would take would be for a lawbreaker to move to another

65

community with a different code of law? Or how would you stop the waste of natural resources by decentralizing the national government? Some company town could strip a national forest clean in the name of the people in that community who depended on that company for their living. They would have the power, and they would destroy the forests. All perfectly legal.

Besides, how would you provide for national security and defense by decentralizing? Do you think the Communists wouldn't like to help themselves to America if they could get it without a war? You need a national military force. You need lots of national agencies to keep a country like this going. If you want to keep your freedoms, you have to do something to protect them. Look around you. Most people today don't have the kind of freedom we have, and their leaders would just as soon take away ours if they could. You just don't understand human nature. You can't eliminate greed or hate or evil by wishing it away or proclaiming a revolution. It takes the kind of loyalty and cooperation Americans have been willing to give.

REVOLUTIONIST: Your trouble is that you are so hung up on the past you don't see what's happening right now. You and your depression and World War II! What's that to us? Why should we have to put up with the kind of world you created just because you tell us that it is the best world available to us? We don't want it, and we won't have it.

OK, we don't have the power, we don't have the guns. But we have a whole lot more. We have a vision of what America can be, and it is a lot different from your holding the line at the status quo. You are so hung up on the past you can't see the full potential in us for creating the kind of life we want now. The Bible says: "The Kingdom of God is within you." That's pretty potent stuff, but it doesn't seem most church people really believe it.

Why not try acting as though God really was inside us? Why not really let the good news soak in? Sure, we don't know exactly how we can do this. Yes, we are vague on our methods for putting the revolution to work. But that is no reason to keep postponing its potential for giving us the kinds of lives we want. You just don't see how bad off we are. You keep telling us to work through the system, Rome wasn't built in a day, and all that. But unless we start the revolution right now, it may be too late. The bombs could go off, the racists could take over, pollution might kill us off. Within a few years it might be all over. That's why we are excited.

But you don't seem to care. You keep telling us to be patient, and we know patience is our worst enemy. So we have to get the message across, and if that means mass demonstrations, even violence, then that is what will be done. Remember, since you like to quote history, all the great revolutions of the past had some violence in them. In a great cause violence can be a truly moral act, a final purging of all the guilt and corruption and compromising and doubt in one's soul in a magnificent gesture of final commitment. We are ready to lay our bodies on the line for the cause. Are you?

TRADITIONALIST: Well, every anarchist in history would vote yes on your proposal. Every person unable to bend the will of the world to his own purposes would shout "amen." It depends on what you want in life. If you want total and unrestricted freedom for individuals to do as they please, then by all means let's purge those who disagree and let the peace and freedom lovers rule the world by themselves. Let them use violence in this one lovely catharsis you talk about, and then return to love, sensitivity, and beauty. Means, you are arguing, are not related to ends. You have no price too high to pay for your revolution.

But you have only faith and no evidence that this is what will happen. What proof do you have that your post-revolutionary world will be better than ours? You really think you can alter human nature. But neither Sigmund Freud nor St. Paul would agree with you. No successful revolutionary leader, like Mao or Castro, would agree with you. Look at the restrictions on freedom in their post-revolutionary countries. Is that your new society? No, thank you!

But let me say you are right in exposing all the phoniness and hypocrisy around today. We have had the double standard for the races; we have been selfish and lax towards the disadvantaged; we have fouled the earth and made a nightmare out of the war in Indochina. But that doesn't automatically mean America is incapable of reform from within. What is it you call it—reordering her priorities?

You talk about the Kingdom of God being within each of us. But what kind of a kingdom was Jesus talking about? Did he promise complete human fulfillment during the lifetime of this planet? Or were there eschatalogical signals in his preachings? I think the latter was the case. Was there a sense in his preaching that man is the master of his own destiny? Or do you get the impression he taught man is subject to a higher law?

And why should God look more favorably on you than on anyone else? I can't find in the Bible anything that makes one group of men so morally superior to others that no one would dare reject their plan of salvation. We are all in this thing together and we have to work it out from that point, and not from some mountaintop vision of the perfect utopia.

Discussion Questions

1. Does history suggest that the turmoil on campus today is more or less one more transitory fad?

2. Why has college education in America traditionally been so oriented toward career preparation? Do you think the kind of inner growth talked about in this section should become the primary concern of college education?

3. Why do so many Americans see the dissenting collegians as not only foolish but as un-American, some suggesting they give aid and comfort to Communism?

4. Why are the campus radicals and racial minorities among the leaders in calling for political and economic decentralization? Are there signs today that decentralization would be the first necessary step to restore the original vision of the Founding Fathers for America?

5. In the United States can highly moral purposes be achieved by the kind of violence discussed in this section?

6. Is the revolutionary vision of the Kingdom of God discussed here harmonious with the New Testament concept of that kingdom?

THE DRAFT AND THE CHURCHES

What limits can be enforced within a nation regarding its authority to require military service of its citizens? How far can the need for loyalty extend into the realm of the rights of the individuals? What role should the churches take in the draft question?

Dialog

TRADITIONALIST: My case won't take very long. Everything in history shows from time immemorial that man needs to defend himself. Show me one instance where two people who really want the same land or resources have not eventually gone to war to get it. Show me further that people have been willing freely to give up those lands and institutions they cherish most deeply. You can't do it.

And take the Bible. It says, "Thou shalt not kill," but it never says you shouldn't defend yourself against those who would destroy you or the Bible. Let's look at Germany in the 1930s. The people, the churches, and the professors really didn't speak up in defense of what they believed in until it was too late and the Nazis had taken over. If they had stopped Hitler in 1933, or if England and France had had the courage to say no to Hitler a few years later, we wouldn't have had World War II and all that destruction.

In the United States one of our great traditions has been strict civilian control over the military. That you can find as early as George Washington. We have seen too much of the disasters in Europe when the military reigned supreme to want that tradition established here. And we have kept that tradition. The final authority has always been the president and the Congress. After every war we dismantled the military as quickly as possible to ensure civilian control. The United States doesn't have gestapos, Siberian concentration camps, or militarist fun and games drummed into the school children, such as you see in China.

We fear the potential loss of freedom, and we pride ourselves on individual liberty. Yet there are times when we have to defend ourselves. We do not want a huge standing army. That is contrary to our traditions as a threat to liberty. But we do need a large army in a time of national peril. So we use the draft; we've used it as far back as the Civil War. We used it in World War I and even before Pearl Harbor and in World War II. With the Communists ready to move in, we keep it operative today.

Yes, many real injustices exist within its operations. It does protect the wealthy college youth, and I'm not so sure seminary students should be exempt. But I'm talking about the basic principle of needing a draft in a free country. I say that if a man is good enough to live in the United States, he is good enough to fight for her. Instead of feeling sorry for himself, the young man ought to be ready to make his contribution to the good of the country which has done so much for him.

It all comes down to survival. If we take away the right to protect ourselves, we won't have anything left. If a young man has any interest in making the future a better place for mankind, he should be willing to make a few sacrifices of his own comfort for that right now.

OK, what about conscientious objectors? What about pacifism? What about objecting to a particular war without objecting to all war? Here is what I think. Everyone who wants to live in the United States should be willing to do what everyone else does here to protect the rights of all of us. That's majority rule. If we didn't have that, we wouldn't have any government at all. And since the military needs all kinds of workers, let's keep on putting the conscientious objectors into those jobs where they won't face actual combat. That policy seems to have worked out well so far. But, let's also be sure everyone does serve his country. No special privileges for anyone.

But I don't buy this idea you can object to just one war but not all wars. In fact the Supreme Court has already ruled on that. The argument stated that Congress did have the constitutional power to enforce draft legislation, and that objections to specific wars must be subordinate to "the Government's interest in procuring the manpower necessary for military purposes, pursuant to the constitutional grant of power to Congress to raise and support armies." That is what I have been trying to say. When you claim individual conscience as an absolute right, you reject the idea of people being able to live together in a community based on shared ideals and common goals. No one has absolute rights.

Besides, look at who the draft dodgers are today and who is supporting them. What more do the Communists want than for the U.S. military to be torn apart at home? That way the Reds win and don't have to lose a life in doing it. Our country, let me repeat, was great by those willing to work hard, by discipline and respect for authority, and real courage for the good of all. Of course, if we don't want that kind of United States, let's start tearing it down now and get back to the caves.

REVOLUTIONIST: Well, now we are at the heart of the problem: patriotism, loyalty, Christian principles. The highest form of patriotism is resistance to the draft. You mention Nazi Germany—fine! If the young men had shown the courage to resist military conscription right there, we would have avoided all the killing. You say the public should have resisted, or France and England should have. But you are treating symptoms; we are dealing with basic causes. No nation can kill or maim or destroy another if it doesn't have the military power to do so.

So, let's start at the beginning, not the end. Let's organize the youth of America and the youth of the world. Without them, the old men wouldn't have anybody to fight their wars unless they wanted to do it themselves! Why should we respect the "wisdom" of our elders when all they can do is get themselves into such a mess that killing is the only way out. Some wisdom!

But you talk about human nature, that man is by nature a predator and something of a beast who needs restraints. Prove it! The fact that humans have been shortsighted or stupid until now doesn't mean they have to be that way. They have been duped by those who want war, or who enjoy killing, or who prefer dictatorships, or who make money from armament makers. The establishment tells people to "kill a commie for Christ" or keep paying taxes for the glory of the motherland, and the people obey. What else could they do, but believe what they were told? They didn't know they didn't have to obey because they didn't believe they could control their own lives.

The leaders didn't want them to know that, so they made up all that patriotism, loyalty, and symbolic ritual stuff to keep the masses quiet. The record doesn't prove man is a hunter; it only proves he hasn't been given a real chance at peace.

On your second point, I agree that the United States does have civilian control over the military. But again, you are arguing from the past and not the present, and that is what we are worried about. Look at the situation right now. The Pentagon and the arms producers have such fantastic economic and political power in this country that no one can control them. We don't dare disarm, not because of the Soviets or the Chinese, but because it might cause a depression, and no political party wants to be blamed for that. And talk about dismantling; today we do have fewer men in uniform than we had in World War II, but the budget for the Pentagon is about two hundred times as large. Some dismantling!

But the real issue is loyalty and the need for self defense. I say that your proposal of non-combatant service for the conscientious objectors is just as immoral as the draft itself. Every person in the military helps those at the killing end. The combat soldiers couldn't do their job if they didn't have the others doing the jobs behind the lines.

Is the conscientious objector who refuses any military service really shirking his duty to his country? I say no. By his willingness to go to jail he is showing how wrong and immoral this country has really become. Someone has to wake up the U.S. before it is too late and we have become a completely militarist state. Someone has to be willing to die for a cause or give up his personal freedom. Isn't that what the first Christians did? Look what happened to their resistance. It didn't die when some were tossed to the lions, but it grew into the most earth-shaking institution the world has known.

That is what the resisters are trying to do—to call Christians and everyone else back to the fundamentals of loyalty to their faith instead of loyalty to any man-made force. That is what America has tried to protect for all these years. That is one big reason why this country never had the military tradition of Europe. Look back at your family tree, especially if your ancestors came to America between 1850, and 1900. Try to find out why they came. I'll bet you most of them came to avoid conscription in their homeland! Did America brand them as disloyal or as traitors? Obviously not. In fact, the draft dodgers were hailed as empire builders, brave pioneers, loyal citizens, and good Americans for coming here!

So I say the draft resisters are the highest patriots; they want to keep the United States loyal to what she stands for. Your generation will never do that, so it is up to us.

TRADITIONALIST: We need to pursue one point further here, the role of the clergy in today's resistance to the draft. What we have in our day when respect for authority and order are being flaunted everywhere, is some of the most respected and influential citizens in our country eagerly telling the youth to break the law. Churches are setting up "draft information" centers, and you don't find any military recruiters being invited there to give their side of the situation. Church conventions pass resolutions condemning war, the draft, the Pentagon, the government, and everything else they don't like.

I'm not for stopping free speech. But I am for fair play, and the clergyman by his commitment to the church is dedicated to justice and fairness. He knows there are at least two sides to every issue, and that you can't make absolute judgments on issues without arrogating the powers of God to yourself. Reinhold Niebuhr said that. If a clergyman really believes in conscientious objection, or some form of nonviolent resistence to the draft, that is his business. But he is also in the business of trying to understand the motives of every other side of an issue and to offer a broad perspective on a moral issue as he can. I don't think our Clergy Concerned are doing a very good job of it.

REVOLUTIONIST: I don't understand. You want the church to speak out on the great issues of the day. Since you quote Niebuhr, let me mention that he was the one who said the civil rights issue taken up by the churches in the mid 1960s saved those churches from total irrelevance. The churches were acting, not just debating. Anyway, why shouldn't the clergy work for those goals they believe in? What is religious commitment all about but a dedication to the highest moral conduct of mankind? Clergymen are not claiming their judgment is infallible when they speak out. They are saying their faith is clear enough on crucial issues to compel them no longer to sit by, but to make as clear as possible what the stakes are in as grave a crisis as the militarist threat in the United States today. Each soul is infinitely precious in the eyes of the Creator. Once you start destroying that vision, you might as well turn the churches over to the government. That is why human welfare must receive the highest priority.

And talk about American traditions. We have separation of church and state; we have the voluntary principle. Those traditions are worth preserving and are worthy of our loyalty. That is what the Clergy Concerned are trying to do. But, you say, they should speak out in a balanced manner, giving all sides. Let me say that there are two things wrong with that. The Pentagon has huge sums of money for propaganda to make its case, and the churches have little or none. And second, a "balanced" approach creates the impression that somewhere between the two poles of opinion the real Christian answer is to be found. I don't believe that, and I don't see why it has to determine what a clergyman or anyone else says on an issue.

Discussion Questions

1. Does American citizenship require some form of military or alternate service from its young adult males?

2. Is America in any real danger of having the military agencies weaken the traditional civilian controls and individual liberty?

3. Is an all-volunteer army harmonious with American ideals about military-civilian relations?

4. Are those who accept jail sentences or leave the country in resistance to the draft a threat to American security? Or are they forerunners of a new idealism which can preserve this nation from internal destruction?

5. Did the nature of the war in Vietnam in itself help encourage the growth of resistance to the draft as compared to the Korean war or World War II? What does this suggest about the long-range implications of abolishing the draft in America?

6. Do clergy have the obligation to present every facet of a major issue such as the draft? Or should they follow the role of advocate?

THE FLAG AND LOYALTY

Is the crisis we face a conflict between those who want to maintain the more traditional forms of national loyalty as opposed to those who seek new expressions and new understandings of America's future? Can as diverse a nation as America maintain its strength so long as its people are so sharply divided over the nature of loyalty to it? Is there a point at which dissent becomes counter-productive? Or does America need persistent self-evaluation as suggested by the radicals?

Dialog

TRADITIONALIST: You know we wouldn't have these problems today—campuses going up in smoke, Congressmen threatened with violence, or youth using up its energy evading the draft—if we could get back to some honest-to-goodness respect for what this country stands for. We have a good thing going here, and we have to keep it that way. Winston Churchill said: "Democracy is the worst form of government except for all the others."

You say you want to save America, and so do I. Remember that this nation was created by those willing to respect what she stood for and worked to improve through legal means when the problems piled up. Loyalty to the country is as old as the Revolutionary War. The patriots then were the ones who "put their bodies on the line" as you like to phrase it. If there hadn't been some real patriotism then, we'd probably still be in the British Empire. That's what I am talking about.

REVOLUTIONIST: I agree, I really do. And when you say, let's get back to some real respect for this country, I agree again. Life, liberty, and the pursuit of happiness, and not the pursuit of the dollar, or the pollution of the land, or the militarizing of the youth or the oppression of the minorities. And we happen to think it can be done. We're not so weighted down by past failures as to be as pessimistic as you seem to be. You think all this has to be done by the book, by the numbers. Do step one, then you can do step two, then on to step three, and presto, a better America. That kind of thinking leaves me cold. We don't think your solutions are going to restore the original promise of America. I've said all that before. What bugs me now is that you feel that unless we do it your way, the job can't be done. You feel that everyone who doesn't march with you, who doesn't wave the flag or support the local police, should be deported.

TRADITIONALIST: Let's stop right there, on that remark about waving the flag. It's all very easy to spout off cliches like that and appear to be very wise. But flying the flag is not the same as the old "my country right or wrong" attitude of a hundred years ago. Sure some people overdid it then on the patriotism kick; if you believed them, you'd think that God wore the stars and stripes.

But that doesn't make the sincere demonstration of national loyalty so rotten today. You say you like commitment. You want people to be honest in expressing just how they feel. So, when some stand up to be counted for the flag, you scorn them. So it seems you are for commitment but only to your approved list of ideals. That is not what freedom of choice is about.

Anyway, the flag. Why do you pick on that for desecration? To me, the abuse shown the flag in the last few years is the same thing as profanity. The burning, the mocking—such as that art show in New York where they made the flag into a sexual symbol—simply show how immature these so called young adults really are, and how poorly prepared they are to save the world. Put it another way. You say we have to be open to each other, to relate honestly and directly by showing respect for each other. Fine, let's do just that. Let's respect the feelings of those who genuinely respect the flag as something extremely important in their lives. They won't bother you when you wear quasi-military clothes to mock the military. So shouldn't you leave them and the flag alone?

How can this country really get back to the fundamentals you talk about and have genuine communication you value so highly as long as you mock its symbols of unity and strength?

Let me make my position as clear as possible. I believe in the proclamation suggested by the *Reader's Digest* (April, 1969) to be read by mayors and governors:

> *Whereas, it has given heart and hope and strength to Americans ever since this nation was born.*
> *Whereas it has flown in times of trouble and in times of triumph as a symbol of America's unquenchable ideals, ever since those ideals were first proclaimed.*
> *Whereas it flies today as a sign that Americans, proud of their country's stirring heritage, are determined to carry the American dream forward.*
> *Let us therefore fly this flag proudly*

Unless we can rally around the flag, or at least avoid desecrating so basic a symbol of national loyalty, we are in for much worse trouble ahead. If you don't love the flag, and that is your choice, at least leave it alone.

REVOLUTIONIST: When you come out for God, country, the flag, and apple pie, you don't leave much room for dissent. You make it sound as though some negative thoughts about Old Glory were the same thing as gross moral turpitude or treason. We do take Old Glory seriously, and we do want to return to the fundamentals. That is why we have to demonstrate to the public how far short we have fallen from our original purposes. People wouldn't pay much attention to our revolution unless we did something dramatic, something that hits them where it hurts. Don't you see? We are trying to help them by making fun of the flag. It is honest, old-fashioned satire, which is protected by freedom of speech. And what is wrong with that? You know the slogan, "It's your Bill of Rights—use it."

You talk about respect for the feelings of others. Well, why can't they respect our feelings? We are as much citizens as they are. We have more at stake, in fact, because we are the future. We want to make it our future.

And isn't all this flag business just a little silly? How much better a patriot are you when you paste your flag decals on windshields or bumpers or use them on stamps? Or run up a flag on your new pole in your front yard? Why not be a true patriot by attacking the real problems facing this country instead of sitting back, flag in hand, and doing nothing?

And don't think a lot of people are making a lot of money from all these flags and pins and decals? The "Spirit of 76" turns out to be a gasoline; companies use red, white, and blue colors for their advertising; you can get furniture now in the colors of Old Glory. And do you think the manufacturer is going to turn over his profits to charity?

But let's compromise. Let's let the courts decide. Should it be a crime to burn the flag, or spit on it, or stomp on it, or use it as a vehicle for free speech?

TRADITIONALIST: Fine, and may I remind you the Supreme Court has done just that. In 1970 New York state won its case against that vulgar use of the flag I mentioned; the ruling made it a crime to dishonor the American Flag in an art display. So you see there are standards that exist. Free speech doesn't mean to say anything you like, and you can't hide under that slogan in your efforts to smear the flag.

REVOLUTIONIST. We will have to agree to disagree there. Let me put it this way. Instead of all these rules about when and how to fly the flag, and all these rites commemorating the past, let's try to live the ideals they represent. Let's not get so bogged down on symbols we forget they are just symbols and not the real thing.

Discussion Questions

1. Is the American flag a symbol of religious as well as nationalist sentiment?

2. Should the flag be protected by law from commercial use as well as from disrespectful use?

3. Should this country develop a new set of symbols to

79

demonstrate her concern for the present rather than in revering the past which to many is so distasteful?

4. When does freedom of speech regarding the flag become abuse of that emblem?

5. Does America need formal patriotic ceremonies and symbols to maintain national unity?

6. Is it feasible to revamp national rites and symbols to divest them of their military overtones and instead invest them with more civilian meanings?

FREE SPEECH AND NATIONAL SECURITY

Americans are justly proud of the free speech clause of the First Amendment, a right enjoyed by very few other peoples in the world. The recent dispute over "The Pentagon Papers" raises several far-reaching issues for our consideration of loyalty: can the voters make informed judgments under a system of classification by which the decision makers can have their mistakes withheld from publication? To what extent should freedoms such as of speech and the press be restricted during times of national emergency? In short, to what should the highest loyalty be given—free speech or national security?

Dialog

TRADITIONALIST: The facts here speak for themselves. The Pentagon papers were stolen by this self-appointed savior of America, Daniel Ellsberg, and then turned over to the press. And the laws on the books at that time strictly barred such activities. Ellsberg knew precisely what he was doing. He knew that official procedures did exist by which classified material could be declassified and made public. But he skipped over all that and gave these reports to the newspapers. We don't know who wrote them; we don't know what their own motives might have been in writing these reports; maybe they withheld some facts, maybe they stretched some facts.

And the newspapers were just as guilty. The editors knew what Ellsberg had done; they knew the laws about classified information. But they went ahead as though it was more important to put the blame for Vietnam on the past administrations than it was to obey the law. And did you see one of the Supreme Court justices stated that the *New York Times* was actually helping to prolong the war by its actions? Their loyalty was strictly to themselves, not for the good of the country.

REVOLUTIONIST: I will start with the facts too. Fact One: nothing in the papers dealt with events in the last four years; it was already history and in no way affected national security. Fact Two: the Nixon administration, just like the Johnson administration had taken *no* step to declassify even one of these items until the *Times* stepped in. Fact Three: did you hear the testimony before Congress by that career expert on classification in which he showed that even typists give automatic classification status to routine documents and that 99.5% of those now given restricted status could safely be made public? Fact Four: never before in American history had a government stepped in to prevent a newspaper from publishing a story. Some call that "prior restraint"; I call it censorship. Why have a First Amendment if the government can ignore it?

TRADITIONALIST: In your list of facts you didn't deny that the papers were stolen. Nor did you deny the right of the government to classify material. Nor did you explain why the *Times* and the other papers appointed themselves to judge whether or not they should obey the laws. Anyway you slice it, these newspapers did commit civil disobedience. They did take it upon themselves to decide what secret information the public should have. They did decide themselves on how much background information and balanced reportage should accompany the documents. They decided themselves that they were better interpreters of the First Amendment than the federal courts. They simply ignored the legal solution of taking their case first to the courts before publishing.

REVOLUTIONIST: Hold it right there! You raise the issue of civil disobedience and loyalty. That is the issue at stake, not one of legal channels or who classifies what. All through American history, those people who wanted to protect the Bill of Rights were willing to do something about their convictions. They were ready to stick their neck out, or rock the boat when that was the only way in which real progress could be made. Don't you see? Ellsberg knew the government would never release documents that would be embarrassing; the public would never have the facts for making sound judgments.

You don't believe me? Did you ever hear of one office holder admit he made the wrong decision? He blames it on someone else, or gets the issues so confused in red tape that the voters don't know who to hold responsible. Have you heard Rusk or Rostow or Bundy or McNamara or Johnson simply come out and say "we erred"? No, you haven't, and you won't. But someone up there did err, and free speech and a free press is the only way we have to learn what did happen. If no one had been willing to break the law, we would be still in the British Empire, or we would still have slavery or racial segregation. Ellsberg knew he was breaking one law, and voluntarily went to jail because he was loyal to a higher tradition in American history, that of the government being responsible to the people.

Discussion Questions

1. Why has the Vietnam war, especially, helped create such distrust by the public of those government leaders who make foreign policy?

2. Do you think Ellsberg is a hero? a criminal? a martyr?

3. Who should decide whether a document endangers national security?

4. Is there a danger today that free speech is being eroded?

5. How can the government restore public confidence in its program of keeping the voters informed?

CONCLUSION

At the outset of this study we raised the question of whether the United States was "coming apart." An attempt was made to suggest certain avenues of thought which might contribute to constructive decisions by the readers. This final section will redefine the general problem of this study in light of what has been said so far and suggest some biblical themes which may continue to inform our judgments.

Having defined the American Creed, the rites of loyalty, and several areas of conflict, we can now raise the question of loyalty in a new manner. To many, perhaps a majority of Americans the fundamental truths of their Creed are something close to permanent dogma. As one commentator said, in a different context: "Conservatives do not deny the existence of undiscovered truths, but they make a critical assumption, which is that those truths that have *already* been apprehended are more important to cultivate than those undisclosed ones . . . Conservatism is the tacit acknowledgement that all that is finally important in human life is behind us; that the crucial explorations have been undertaken, and that it is given to man to know what are the great truths that emerged from them. Whatever is to come cannot outweigh the importance of what has gone before".[1] That statement could well stand as the credo of the Traditionalist whose opinions were summarized in this chapter.

On the other hand, especially among younger citizens, the fundamental truths of the American Creed may well have been satisfactory and even noble at the time of their occurrence in history. But, our young adults charge, those doctrines should not have such authority to bind those living now and in the future simply because at one time they were so important. The Revolutionist, whose ideas we summarized, would agree with the following commentator as to the essence of change: "That quality I would define as concern with process rather than product . . . as concern with the manner of handling experience or materials rather than with the experience of materials themselves."[2] By that he meant, America "is not a fixed or an immutable ideal toward which the citizens of this nation strive. America is process."

To sum up this point, the Traditionalist would absorb all new insights into his system which he feels reflects as much transcendent truth as is humanly possible. To him this truth is already apprehended and understood. The Revolutionist, holding to process, remains open to new truths and insights which may well require equally fundamental changes in the fabric of his society. This is not to say that the Traditionalist is "closeminded," nor that the Revolutionist has no concept of permanent truth. It is rather, in our case, a matter of whether society's best interests are served by adhering as closely as possible to those tested ideals of the past, and in so doing trim and fit the present demand for reform into that pattern. Or, whether human experience is such that no past solution or commitment is necessarily adequate to cope with the full range of human potential for the future.

One bumper sticker says: Honor America. This means, honor its past accomplishments and ideals and thus gain control over the flux of the present. Another sticker reads: America — Love It and Live It. This means that implementing national ideals cannot be restricted to following past solutions but can be expressed in a manner meaningful for today.

Since I talked earlier about the either/or fallacy between our debaters, I must not fall into the same trap. Most Americans are not completely in one of these two camps. But the two extremes have been defined in this particular manner so that the wide range of options existing in the middle is made more clear.

Our second task is to explore biblical resources available for preserving that which still seems strong in the American tradition, while moving to the sidelines those themes which no longer seem to serve us well. We remember, as a starter, that all human institutions are under the judgment of God. When we invoke the name of God into our patriotic observances, it would be well to remember that fact and avoid the identification of national will with the purposes of the Almighty. Americans are especially vulnerable at this point with their sense of sacred mission and being the last, best hope. Yet God punished the original chosen people and destroyed their idols.

Beyond that, under God's judgment there is also the ongoing need for both the Traditionalist and the Revolutionist to recognize the elusiveness of any easily achieved consensus. In fact, one probably should be downright suspicious of any quick rapport. It may well be as the Traditionalist hopes that all this dissent is just one more passing fad. But it may also be true as the Revolutionist argues that Americans are moving into an entirely new phase of history as far reaching as the Reformation. Thus, swift and easy answers are not going to be plentiful this season.

Third, the Christian understanding of the springs of human behavior should prepare him to avoid either the seductive calls of cynicism leading to despair over any improvement; or to a commitment to revolution through man-made processes which cuts itself off from its ultimate source of life. One finds no biblical guarantee of hell or heaven on this earth or in this lifetime. Recognizing this, one can better withstand the many disappointments over our many failures, without becoming blind to the many opportunities for establishing liberty and justice for all in the here and now. This is another way of starting with faith, hope, and love.

NOTES

PREFACE

1. Richard Hofstadter and Michael Wallace, eds., *American Violence: A Documented History* (New York: Random House Vintage Books, 1971).

CHAPTER 1

1. Daniel B. Stevick, *Civil Disobedience and the Christian* (New York: Seabury Press, 1969), p. 23.

2. Thomas Sanders, *Protestant Concepts of Church and State* (New York: Holt, Rinehart, & Winston, 1964), pp. 23-48.

CHAPTER 2

1. Gunnar Myrdal, *An American Dilemma: The Negro Problem and Modern Democracy* (New York: Harper and Row Torchbooks, 1944, 1962), 1:3.

2. Sidney Mead, *The Lively Experiment: The Shaping of Christianity in America* (New York: Harper and Row, 1963), ch. 7.

3. A very readable summary is in Marty E. Marty, *Righteous Empire: The Protestant Experience in America* (New York: The Dial Press, 1970).

4. See Norman Graebner, ed., *Manifest Destiny* (Indianapolis: The Bobbs-Merrill Company, 1968).

5. W. Lloyd Warner, *American Life: Dream and Reality* (Chicago: University of Chicago Press Phoenix Books, rev. ed., 1962), pp. 20-23.

6. Louis L. Snyder, ed., *The Dynamics of Nationalism* (Princeton, N.J.: D. Van Nostrand Co., Inc., 1964), p. 274.

7. *Ibid.,* 279.

8. Russell B. Nye, *This Almost Chosen People* (East Lansing: Michigan State University Press, 1966), p. 168.

CHAPTER 3

1. University of Chicago Press, 1956.

2. *Ibid.,* p. 6.

3. *Ibid.,* p. 30.

4. Carlton J. H. Hayes, *Nationalism and Religion* (New York: Macmillan Co., 1960), ch. 1.

5. *Ibid.,* p. 167.

6. Warner, *American Life: Dream and Reality*, ch. 1.

7. Conrad Cherry, ed., *God's New Israel: Religious Interpretations of American Destiny* (Englewood Cliffs, N.J.: Prentice-Hall, 1971), p. 6.

8. For amplification, see Robert N. Bellah, "Civil Religion in America," in Bellah and William G. McLoughlin, eds., *Religion in America* (Boston: Beacon Press, 1968), pp. 3-23; and comments on it in Elwyn A. Smith, ed., *The Religion of the Republic* (Philadelphia: Fortress Press, 1971), chs. 1 and 11.

CHAPTER 4

1. Erling Jorstad, *The Politics of Doomsday: Fundamentalists of the Far Right* (Nashville: Abingdon Press, 1970), pp. 38-44.

2. Graham, "Satan's Religion," *American Mercury*, August, 1954, 74:41-46.

3. See the list in Jorstad, *Politics of Doomsday*, p. 159.

CHAPTER 5

1. Reprinted from *Up From Liberalism* by William F. Buckley Jr., published by Arlington House, New Rochelle, New York, and used with permission.

2. John A. Kouwenhoven, "What's American About America?," *The Beer Can by the Highway* (New York: Doubleday and Company, 1961), pp. 66, 72-73. Copyright by Doubleday and Company, Inc., and used with permission.

FOR FURTHER READING

In addition to the titles mentioned in the footnotes, the following are suggested to those wishing to read more.

* Denotes a book specifically suited for congregational discussion.

* Bennett, John C. *When Christians Make Political Decisions.* New York: Association Press, 1964.

    A sober, penetrating explanation of the relationships between Christian social ethics and American citizenship by a famed teacher.

* Council for Christian Social Action, United Christian Church. *America's Culture Religion and the Churches.* 289 Park Avenue South, New York, 10010.

    A brief, helpful summary on how aspects of American religious life are identical with its secular culture.

Specific congregational programs for constructive action are presented.

Foster, Julian, and Long, Durward, eds., *Protest! Student Activism in America*. New York: William Morrow and Co., 1970.

A long, complete anthology of primary sources illustrating the many facets to this movement. Several case studies help give this reader a sense of reality missing in most other readers on this subject.

Gabriel, Ralph Henry. *Traditional Values in American Life*. New York: Harcourt, Brace, 1963.

A distinguished teacher explains the origins and durability of the American Creed.

Gentles, Frederick, and Steinfeld, Melvin. *Dream on, America: A History of Faith and Practice*. San Francisco, Canfield Press, Harper and Row, Publishers, 1971, 2 vols.

The most thorough textbook discussion of the American Creed. Highly recommended.

Greeley, Andrew M. *Come Blow Your Mind with Me: Provocative Reflections on the American Religious Scene*. New York: Doubleday and Co., 1971.

Several readable, penetrating surveys of today's issues, with special emphasis on the Roman Catholic world. Hard cover.

Howe, Louise Kapp., ed. *The White Majority: Between Poverty and Affluence*. New York: Vintage Books, 1971.

Very helpful essays by experts on the crises facing the blue collar workers; deals with politics, religion, attitude towards dissent, blacks, law and order and other related subjects.

* Kirk, Russell. *The American Cause*. Chicago: Henry Regnery Co., 1957.

A useful summary of the major issues discussed by one of the leading political conservatives in America.

Lemon, Richard. *The Troubled American*. New York: Simon and Schuster, 1970.

A summary of several national public opinion polls taken on the problems facing Americans today; discussed are racism, war, dissent, welfare, police, among other issues. Provides good documentation to the theories. Hard cover.

* Skolnick, Jerome H., ed. *The Politics of Protest*. New York: Clarion Books, 1969.

Perceptive, interpretive essays on the whole range of current crises in America produced for the National Commission on the Causes and Prevention of Violence.

Swomley, John M., Jr. *American Empire: The Political Ethics of Twentieth Century Conquest*. New York: Macmillan, 1970.

Highly stimulating and controversial interpretations of American foreign policy since 1900 from the perspective of a teacher of Christian social ethics.

Zinn, Howard. *Disobedience and Democracy: Nine Fallacies on Law and Order*. New York: Vintage Books, 1968.

Argues in concrete terms how the national and state governments are weakening traditional American respect for law and order by their policies of law enforcement in our times.